PROPHET T.B. JOSHUA

the mirror

THE MIRROR SHOWS US WHO WE WERE, WHO WE ARE AND WHO WE SHALL BE.

Author's Comment

God chooses the grace rather than works (Ep2v8-9)
This means if the weak come to HIM HE would help
their weakness Just as HE would help the strong.
God knows we are weak. that is why HE
chooses grace

    If God had chosen works rather than grace
man would have the autonomy to Choose whom
to help with his works and how to do his works
the battle would be for the strongest leaving
no room for people like me (I B Joshua)
The race would be for the swiftest leaving
no room for people like Me (I B Joshua)

PROPHET T.B. JOSHUA

THE MIRROR
PROPHET T.B. JOSHUA

A SCOAN Production 2006

ISBN 0-620-37453-5

Reach us on the Internet:
www.scoan.com

DEDICATION

This book is dedicated to all children of God who are fighting without but filled with fear within. Elisha said to his servant: " 'Do not fear, for those who are with us are more than those who are with them'." 2 KINGS 6:16 NKJV

Nevertheless, I say to you that those that are fighting for you, protecting you and taking care of you are more than the forces of the adversary.

As you read this book, I pray for you as Elisha prayed for his servant: "Lord Jesus, open their understanding, so they will doubt no more, worry and fear no more. Open their hearts to faith, in Your holy name we pray. Amen."

Believe Someone is working out the answer.

TABLE OF CONTENTS

INTRODUCTION

God's genera   n this book mirror God and we see in them the image and likeness of God. They are men and women of faith who share in the authority and power of our God over all forms of satanic oppression:

"I have given you authority to trample on snakes and scorpions and to overcome all the power of the enemy; nothing will harm you." LUKE 10:19

Our Lord, Jesus Christ, is disappointed that men lack the necessary faith to release the power that has been given them.

Abraham
GENESIS 22:1-18

abraham

Our duty is to obey God's instructions. His duty is to keep His promise.

GENESIS 22:1-18

"Some time later God tested Abraham. He said to him, 'Abraham!' 'Here I am,' he replied. Then God said, 'Take your son, your only son, Isaac, whom you love, and go to the region of Moriah. Sacrifice him there as a burnt offering on one of the mountains I will tell you about.' ...Then he reached out his hand and took the knife to slay his son. But the angel of the LORD called out to him from heaven, 'Abraham! Abraham!' 'Here I am,' he replied. 'Do not lay a hand on the boy,' he said. 'Do not do anything to him. Now I know that you fear God, because you have not withheld from me your son, your only son'. " GENESIS 22:1-2, 10-12

Father Abraham did not allow his love for Isaac, his only son, to affect his relationship with God, knowing that the purpose of his own life was beyond his love for Isaac. The pain of sacrificing his only son did not affect his relationship with God. He knew that the purpose of life was beyond the pain and joy of life. When you glorify the Creator rather than the created, you live each day to overcome. I mean, you will live above human destruction.

Imagine what would have happened to Abraham if he had waited for a more convenient time to carry out God's instruction. We know it was not convenient for Abraham to sacrifice his only son – Isaac, just as it is not convenient for anyone to give out the only possession he has.

"Then God said, 'Take your son, your only son, Isaac, whom you love, and go to the region of Moriah. Sacrifice him there as a burnt offering on one of the mountains I will tell you about'. " GENESIS 22:2

The Bible says, "whom you love" (not "whom you hate"). You know you have many children. There are some of your children of whom you would say, "I don't want to hear about that boy. He's a trouble-maker. He's stubborn."

Suppose Abraham had waited for a more convenient day to carry out God's instruction, what would have happened to him? As we know, it was not convenient for him to take his only beloved son for sacrifice, as it is not convenient for anyone to take his only beloved son for sacrifice. If Abraham's belief did not see beyond Isaac, he would not have had the courage to obey God's instruction. You need to remember that **our duty is to obey God's instructions. His duty is to keep His promise**. The way of obedience is the way of blessing.

The expression, "Here I am", means, "I am all Yours". "Your will is my command." "Lord I am committed to You, whatever You ask me, I will do" (see GENESIS 22:1).

If you were sent to unpleasant places, would you go? Abraham was ready to carry out not only pleasant instructions but also painful ones. Are you, however, ready to go to unpleasant places today? I mean a place of sacrifice. People want to go to places of reward rather than of sacrifice. Today, people show less interest for things of the Spirit, which cannot be quantified in terms of position, money and physical reward. Placed in the same condition as Abraham, you would likely say, "Here I am, send me, but how much will You give me?" You would want to know how much money, position or any other physical reward you would gain after carrying out the instructions.

Listen to Abraham: "Here I am; I am all Yours. Your will is my command; I am committed to You, Lord. Whatever You ask me to do, I will do."

He was not saying he would be ready only to follow pleasant instructions; whether pleasant or painful, he was ready. When I say I have faith in God, I mean I have confidence in Him; I believe in Him; I obey all His commands, I mean I am committed to Him, I know Him.

PRAYER POINTS

Ask God to fill your heart with the Spirit of obedience, in Jesus' name.

Say, "Lord, I'm ready to do Your will and to obey Your Words. Jesus, I want to be a doer of Your Words, in Your holy name."

Lord Jesus, I am giving up to Your will.
I have given up to Your will.
I am ready to go wherever You want me to go;
to say whatever You want me to say;
to be whatever You want me to be.
I am ready Lord; I am ready now!
The time is short – the world is coming to an end.
I don't want to waste my time.
I am ready to evangelise Your message,
all over the world, by myself, if necessary.
I'm ready; I'm ready now – let's go God!

STUDY QUESTIONS

ONE// In any true relationship, each party should be ready to make some sacrifice in order to keep the relationship going. What sacrifice are you making in order to maintain your relationship with Jesus?

TWO// What made Abraham say, "...I and the boy will go over there. We will worship and then we will come back to you..." if he knew that he had to sacrifice Isaac? (see GENESIS 22:5)

THREE// The cost of disobedience is far greater than the cost of obedience. What would have happened if Abraham had not obeyed God's instruction?

FOR FURTHER READING

ROMANS 8:25

HEBREWS 11:17-19

DEUTERONOMY 7:9

ISAIAH 6:8

JOHN 15:14

"talk what you believe // WHAT YOU BELIEVE"
WORDS TO MEDITATE ON DAY AND NIGHT//PROPHET
MEDITATION BRINGS REVELATION//T.B. JOSHUA

"Faith focuses on Jesus Christ and His sufficiency." // GENESIS 13:14-17

"Faith is the certainty of God's yet unfulfilled promises." // HEBREWS 6:15

"To bring God's promises to reality is by faith." // ROMANS 4:16

"Faith in Christ Jesus is a necessary condition. I mean a condition that must be met." // GENESIS 15:6

"God keeps using // GENESIS 15:5
everything HE has made.
HE used the stars to
motivate Abraham's
faith for children. HE
used clay. HE used a fish
to give Peter the money.
HE used water to turn a
marriage into a place
of miracle."

"If I say I have faith // HEBREWS 11:8-10
in God, I mean I have
confidence in Him, I
know Him, I believe in
Him, I am committed to
Him and I obey all
His commands."

Joseph
GENESIS 37, 39-42

joseph

When you are conscious of your dream, whatever the situation and whatever happens on the outside will not matter to you.

GENESIS 37, 39-42

"Now Joseph had a dream, and he told it to his brothers; and they hated him even more. So he said to them, 'Please hear this dream which I have dreamed: There we were, binding sheaves in the field. Then behold, my sheaf arose and also stood upright; and indeed your sheaves stood all around and bowed down to my sheaf.' And his brothers said to him, 'Shall you indeed reign over us? Or shall you indeed have dominion over us?' So they hated him even more for his dreams and for his words." GENESIS 37:5-8 NKJV

Sometimes you see people are happy, whereas there is nothing to be happy about on the outside. This is because they have a dream, which is known to them alone. This was the case with Joseph.

"So it came to pass, when Joseph had come to his brothers, that they stripped Joseph of his tunic, the tunic of many colours that was on him. Then they took him and cast him into a pit. And the pit was empty; there was no water in it." GENESIS 37:23-24 NKJV

Even when he was right in the pit, he was not overwhelmed by sadness, fear or doubts. His condition in the dry pit could not derail him because his focus was on his dream, not on the pit condition.

"So Joseph found favour in his sight, and served him. Then he made him overseer of his house, and all that he had he put under his authority. So it was, from the time that he had made him overseer of his house and all that he had, that the LORD blessed the Egyptian's house for Joseph's sake; and the blessing of the LORD was on all that he had in the house and in the field." GENESIS 39:4-5 NKJV

Even when he was in Potiphar's house where he was well cared for, his focus remained on his dream. While he was enjoying all the favours, he still believed that his dream was greater than his present enjoyment.

"Then Joseph's master took him and put him into the prison, a place where the king's prisoners were confined. And he was there in the prison." GENESIS 39:20 NKJV

Then he went to jail. While in prison, his focus was on his dream, not on his prison condition. Many today are overwhelmed by the situation around them because they do not focus on their dreams. When you are conscious of your dream, whatever the situation and whatever happens on the outside will not matter to you.

Remember, we do not look at what is seen but what is unseen, for what is seen is temporary while what is unseen is permanent. As children of God, we walk by faith, not by sight. We therefore are not overwhelmed by what is seen. Joseph was in the prison but he did not allow the prison conditions to overwhelm him. Instead, he looked through the window, saw beautiful skies and gave thanks to God, and said, "Thank You, Jesus!" He never looked down. **Getting you to look at life, its storms and adversities from the human point of view is a trap from satan.** I mean looking at your situation from the human point of view (i.e., on the outside), will give you discouragement, fear, doubt and anxiety.

Joseph had a dream when he was very small. He saw stars bow before him (see GENESIS 37:9). That was the dream he followed; that was his focus. He held onto that ever since. Whatever the situation, the Bible says, Joseph always said to himself, "This is not where I belong." The future I desire is a beautiful picture. My words must be the photograph of that future I desire. My action, behaviour, way of life and everything about me must be the photograph of the future I desire.

Each time Joseph found himself in a place, which was contrary to his vision, he would say to himself, "I know where I belong - not here!" When he was in the dry pit, he said to himself, "I know where I belong

- not here!" That imparted into him the strength to endure the condition in the dry pit. When he found himself in prison, he said to himself, "I know where I belong – not here!" That imparted into him the strength to endure the condition of the prison. When he found himself in the situation of condemnation, where Potiphar's wife was trying to tempt him, the Bible says, he had three reasons why he did not yield to the temptation of Potiphar's wife:

ONE// he considered who he was,
TWO// he was a covenant child, and,
THREE// he was a child with the promise of God.

If you are a man of vision, you will be able to know where you belong. Indeed, you should be able to know where you belong! When Joseph found himself in the dry pit, he said to himself, "This is not God's promise. Where I am going, there is something greater. I know where I belong – not here!" The Bible says, he continued to endure. Remember, **our trouble becomes easier to handle when we know that it will not last long.** He knew that he would be in a dry pit for a short time. Whatever the trouble was, it would be for a short time. When he was in the prison, he knew the condition there was for a short time.

If you know where you belong, why do you complain? Why do you fight? Why do you have time for every unnecessary question? Why? Why do you bother about what people say about you? Why do you turn into a beggar when you know where you belong?

Joseph knew where he belonged. If it were not so, he would have thought he would die in the dry pit. He would have fallen into self-pity, "Why God? Why me? Why me!" As he knew where he belonged, he looked around and said, "I know where I belong – not here! I will not die. I shall live to see the glory of God!" He was going to the throne.

If he had had no dream, he would have died in the dry pit. When he was in the dry pit, he said to himself, "This is not where I belong." You can be content, no matter what happens to you on the outside. Whatever happens on the outside does not determine whether or not you have a contented life.

When God puts something in your mind, the circumstances, what people say or what happens around you, cannot change your mind. Remember, it was what God put in Joseph's mind that was his focus when he was in the dry pit, in the prison yard and in Potiphar's house.

God sometimes uses hard times to draw us to Himself, so that we can take our proper position and possession in Him. For instance, at the time Joseph had the dream of his future, he was too young to appreciate the glory that was ahead of him – how he would become the prime minister. I mean if he had become the prime minister earlier than he did in Egypt, he would have been too inexperienced to handle the position. So, the hard times he went through in the dry pit, in Potiphar's house and in the prison, were God's own way of preserving him for the glory ahead. If Joseph had not been in the prison, he would not have had the contact that finally linked him to the throne in Egypt. It was in these dark periods of his life that he gained the necessary experience and maturity to handle the responsibilities imposed on him by the exalted position he occupied in the royal court in Egypt. From this, we can understand that God sometimes uses hard times – that is, unpleasant situations – to preserve us so that we can take our future in our hands.

"Joseph said to them, 'Do not be afraid, for am I in the place of God? But as for you, you meant evil against me; but God meant it for good, in order to bring it about as it is this day, to save many people alive'. "
GENESIS 50:19-20 NKJV

Sometimes God allows poverty so that you can take your proper position and possession. Suffering, sickness and loneliness can preserve one. **God visits His people with hard times so that they may learn His way.** His way, though hard to the ungodly man, is desirable and profitable because it leads us to safety and eternal life.

Remember, if we go through hard times, we will be able to recognise and appreciate freedom. Your toiling, struggling and working hard may be to make you see and appreciate freedom when it finally comes.

PRAYER POINTS

When Joseph was in the dry pit, he kept saying, "This is not where I belong." He was able to endure that dry pit. You have lost focus, that is why poverty can make you cry. God will bring that revelation back. When you have a revelation, you will be content. As a result of this dream, he was able to withstand the situation in the dry pit and in the prison.

All you need are His mercy and favour. Do you want a good life? You must believe. The future you desire does not permit you to doubt or fear.

Ask God to give you the words of the future you desire, in Jesus' name.

In the mighty name of Jesus Christ, receive the future you desire!

STUDY QUESTIONS

ONE// How do you think Joseph managed to remain humble after his promotion as ruler over all the land of Egypt?

TWO// How did Joseph know that the dream he had was from God and was for his future - not just merely a product of his own thoughts and imaginations?

THREE// In GENESIS 42, we see Joseph in a position of influence. How did he become influential?

FOR FURTHER READING

JAMES 1:12

ACTS 27:25

PHILIPPIANS 4:11

PSALM 118:17

PSALM 69:32-33

talk

"talk what you believe // WHAT YOU BELIEVE"

WORDS TO MEDITATE ON DAY AND NIGHT//PROPHET
MEDITATION BRINGS REVELATION//T.B. JOSHUA

"Faith is a firm // HEBREWS 10:23
expectation that God
will perform all HE has
promised us in Christ
Jesus."

"Patience, perseverance, // JAMES 1:2-4
endurance, forbearance
are the tools, the
instruments, for a man
of faith."

"If your belief cannot // LUKE 16:10-12
see beyond the position
you occupy now as a
cleaner, as a housemaid
or as a follower, how
can you see beyond
your position when you
become a manager, a
master or a leader?"

david

It was God's Word, which came out I SAMUEL 17:32-52 **of David's lips, that produced an overcoming spirit in him.**

"David said to the Philistine, 'You come against me with sword and spear and javelin, but I come against you in the name of the LORD Almighty, the God of the armies of Israel, whom you have defied. This day the LORD will hand you over to me, and I'll strike you down and cut off your head. Today I will give the carcasses of the Philistine army to the birds of the air and the beasts of the earth, and the whole world will know that there is a God in Israel. All those gathered here will know that it is not by sword or spear that the LORD saves; for the battle is the LORD's, and He will give all of you into our hands'. "
I SAMUEL 17:45-47

David spoke the Word of Faith and the giant fell. Faith acts on God's Word. It believes now; it receives now; it acts now. When we take God at His Word, that Word will stand good in the trial. God's Word is Spirit; it is light where there is darkness, an understanding where there is ignorance and an awareness of righteousness where there is sin. It shows us who we were, who we are and who we shall be. It shows us the mercy and justice of the Lord and, above all, the joys of salvation and the agony of hell. A Christian must speak the Word of Faith at all times (see COLOSSIANS 4:6).

It was God's Word, which came out of David's lips, that produced an overcoming spirit in him. He spoke the Word of Faith and the giant fell. Victory is in our faith. Power and protection are in our faith.

Confess what you believe and believe what you confess. Righteousness is for all that believe in their heart that Jesus is our Saviour. Victory is for all that believe in their heart that Jesus is our Redeemer. Imagine what would have happened if David had not spoken the Word of Faith in his encounter with Goliath. Imagine the destruction he would have invited to himself and the people of Israel:

ONE// God would not have heard him,
TWO// he would have been destroyed in the hands
of Goliath, and,
THREE// the people of Israel would have been routed.

If he had not spoken the Word of Faith, his word would have been not only idle but also very destructive. His people looked on to see what would become of the small David after his encounter with Goliath. Among them were his relations, friends, enemies as well as those who believed in him and those who did not; they were all watching to see the outcome of his faith. Now at the battlefield, if what David spoke with his mouth were not what he believed in his heart, one could only imagine what would have become of him when he was face to face with the giant. His word would have been idle, meaningless and, at that point, destructive. When you are face to face with Jesus, HE is not interested in your attire, position, size or your political and economic power. I mean HE is not interested in your power on the outside but in your faith because faith is what makes you one with Him.

Jesus said, "If you have faith in Me, these works that I do, you will do also – even more" (see JOHN 14:12).

This means with faith, His power, ability and strength become yours – that is what makes you one with Him.

Faith: with faith, you are justified; you are no longer condemned. **With faith, the mountain of guilt which had separated you from God will be removed, thus making you one with Him – thus making you a child of God.**

If David were not a man of faith, he would have considered the size of the giant and he would have been intimidated by the size and armour of his adversary. Remember, the giant was better armed than David was in the physical. Apart from his size, Goliath had a spear, javelin, machete and a shield as against the small David, barely armed, with a simple sling. Remember, his own people doubted him; that was why they went to the king.

If David were to look at the intimidating size of Goliath,

he would have given in to the giant's threats. In the physical, Goliath was better armed and experienced in matters of warfare.

On the outside, Goliath created a feeling of intimidation and fear in people – this was the weapon he carried; but David, as a man of faith, triumphed over him because his weapon was on the inside. David's ability was on the inside – it was the power of God. This is what is meant by: "In our hearts we believe; with our mouths we confess."

Power on the outside (that is, intimidation and threats) was the weapon of Goliath but David's weapon was on the inside. There was power in his mouth; the belief in his heart was released by faith out of his mouth. He confessed victory and victory was his lot. Here is how David released the belief in his heart by faith out of his mouth:

"David said to the Philistine, 'You come against me with sword and spear and javelin, but I come against you in the name of the LORD Almighty, the God of the armies of Israel, whom you have defied'." I SAMUEL 17:45

David spoke the Words of Faith and the giant fell. This means David spoke with his mouth what he believed in his heart. **It takes faith to achieve victory. After the victory is won, anyone can shout, "Hallelujah!" "Amen!" "Hosanna!"**

"David ran and stood over him. He took hold of the Philistine's sword and drew it from the scabbard. After he killed him, he cut off his head with the sword. When the Philistines saw that their hero was dead, they turned and ran. Then the men of Israel and Judah surged forward with a shout and pursued the Philistines to the entrance of Gath and to the gates of Ekron..." I SAMUEL 17:51-52

It did not take his people any faith, to shout, "Thank You," when the giant fell. Nevertheless, David spoke the Words of Faith before the giant fell. So also, anyone can shout after a miracle has happened but it takes faith to shout before the miracle happens.

PRAYER POINTS

In the natural, David could not withstand the giant because the giant was mighty in nature and mighty

in body. David was very small. This shows that we are not fighti a natural situation. A believer who operates in la ral has no power.

By the power that gave victory to David, the Lord should give you victory, in Jesus' name!

Continue to speak the Word of Faith to your giant, "Move in the mighty name of Jesus Christ!"

STUDY QUESTIONS

ONE// Imagine that you were in the position of David where those in authority, your colleagues and even your brothers, did not believe in you. Would you allow their opinions to change your opinion of yourself?

TWO// Giants cannot kill you but the fear of giants can (see JUDGES 7:12-22). What is your giant? Is it sickness, anxiety, poverty or setback? Remember, if David had considered the size of the giant, he would have been scared to submission. How are you looking at your present situation?

THREE// David spoke the Words of Faith and the giant

fell. When you are faced with a giant - sickness, trial, crisis, temptation, etc., what kind of words do you use?

FOUR// David acknowledged God for all HE had done for him in the past. Do you still acknowledge God? Do you acknowledge His goodness when you were yet small, when you were in your mother's womb (see I SAMUEL 17:37) ?

FOR FURTHER READING

ROMANS 10:10-11

2 CORINTHIANS 4:13

PSALM 19:14

I SAMUEL 16:10-13

2 CORINTHIANS 6:7

talk

"talk what you believe//WHAT YOU BELIEVE

WORDS TO MEDITATE ON DAY AND NIGHT//**PROPHET**
MEDITATION BRINGS REVELATION//**T.B. JOSHUA**
"

"A man of faith is a man // ACTS 13:22
with a difference."

"Belief in Christ Jesus // EPHESIANS 6:16-17
is a prerequisite for the
battle against satan."

"Faith is a force that // ISAIAH 55:11
moves our words
to work."

"Faith is the cause of // I JOHN 5:4
victory, the means, the
instrument, the spiritual
armour by which we
overcome sin and
the world."

"The belief in our heart // I SAMUEL 17:26, 45-50
can only be expressed
by faith."

"You know HE will // I SAMUEL 17:24-26, 50
not leave you without
victory. Stop discussing
your battle."

"When you know that // I SAMUEL 17:45
the One inside you is
the One behind you,
nothing on the outside
will matter to you."

"You can only show who // ACTS 16:16-18
you are in Christ Jesus
when you speak with
your mouth what you
believe in your heart."

The Shunammite Woman
2 KINGS 4: 20-26

the shunam-mite

It does not take long to realise that Jesus believes what you say is important.

woman
2 KINGS 4: 20-26

"Please run now to meet her, and say to her, 'Is it well with you? Is it well with your husband? Is it well with the child?' And she answered, 'It is well'. "
2 KINGS 4:26 NKJV

A dead child was being kept in the room but she answered, "Everything is alright – it is well." And when you read the passage further, you will see that it was alright indeed – it was well indeed.

What you say before meeting a man of God sometimes

becomes true after meeting him.

God needs to grant you the grace to speak His Word with boldness. You need to speak the Words of God with boldness. The Psalmist says, "Even though I walk through the valley of the shadow of death, I will fear no evil..." PSALM 23:4

"It is well with me. It is well and so shall it be." When you look at the book of 2 KINGS 4:20, the only child that this woman had, died. The woman kept the child in the room and went to meet Prophet Elisha. On her way, she met the servant and the servant said, "What is happening to you, madam? How is your son? How is your husband? How are you?" Instead of saying, "My only child died", she simply said to the servant, "It is well," and it was well indeed.

There is power in your mouth. The belief in your heart is released by faith out of your mouth. It does not take long to realise that Jesus believes what you say is important. Your words will either justify or condemn you. You shall account for the words spoken by your mouth (see MATTHEW 12:36-37). If they are not according to the truth of God's Word, they will be idle, meaningless and oftentimes destructive. What a person says with his mouth can either release or obstruct the passage of what he believes in his heart.

For this reason, whenever it looks like things are working against you, start confessing the Words of Faith. Learn to say, "It is well", and it shall be well indeed, in Jesus' name. Amen.

PRAYER POINTS

Whenever it looks like things are working against you, start confessing the Words of Faith. Learn to say, "It is well", and it shall be well, in Jesus' name.

If the evidence of what you believe is your faith in God's Word, receive more now! Believe now and act now, in Jesus' name.

STUDY QUESTIONS

ONE// Why did the Shunammite woman put the boy's

dead body on the bed of the prophet? What was her belief?

TWO// For anyone to say, "It is well", when crises like death comes, what can you say about this?

THREE// Why was Elisha inside the room alone with the dead body? What could have happened that his only disciples could not enter? Who would have been his witness?

FOUR// The example of the Shunammite woman shows that we have power in our mouths. As Christians, what then do we need to release that power?

FOR FURTHER READING

2 CORINTHIANS 4:13

MATTHEW 12:33-37

PROVERBS 18:20-23

JAMES 3:1-18

"talk what you believe//WHAT YOU BELIEV
WORDS TO MEDITATE ON DAY AND NIGHT//PROPHET
MEDITATION BRINGS REVELATION//T.B. JOSHUA"

"Don't tell me what you   // 2 KINGS 4:26
   feel; tell me what you
      know; tell me what
         you believe."

"Faith requires you to   // I KINGS 18:41-46
   speak out before you
      feel or see them."

"In the face of trouble,   // 2 KINGS 4:26
talk what you believe."

"It is true we have the // PROVERBS 13:2
things we believe
and speak."

"The Words of Faith are // ROMANS 10:8-10
in two places:
in our hearts we believe
and in our mouths
to confess."

job

Your belief should be based on something beyond your present situation. JOB 1:18-22

"While he was still speaking, yet another messenger came and said, 'Your sons and daughters were feasting and drinking wine at the oldest brother's house, when suddenly a mighty wind swept in from the desert and struck the four corners of the house. It collapsed on them and they are dead, and I am the only one who has escaped to tell you!' At this, Job got up and tore his robe and shaved his head. Then he fell to the ground in worship and said: 'Naked I came from my mother's womb, and naked I will depart. The LORD gave and the LORD has taken away; may the name of the LORD be praised.' In all this, Job did not sin by charging God with wrongdoing." JOB 1:18-22

Assuming his confidence was based on wealth, position, power, might and children (these physical things), he would have lost his confidence when they were taken from him. His confidence remained even stronger without them because it was born of faith.

Job's belief saw beyond his earthly possessions that were destroyed – his children, cattle and camels. Even all of his body was full of sores. If his belief did not see beyond his possessions, he would not have had the courage or hope to be firm in his faith. The Bible says he was firm. If he had seen his possessions as the basis of his relationship with God, he would not have had anything to rest his faith on when they were taken away. But he did not count on his possessions or social relations as the basis of his relationship with God (see JOB 1:20). Job's belief was based on something beyond the sores and boils that covered his skin. Your belief should be based on something beyond your present situation.

The Bible says that Job did not blame God for his situation; rather, he was ready to die. This means he saw his hard times as a reason for believing in God, just as he had seen good times as a reason for believing in God as well.

In our weakness, the strength of God quickens and energizes us. Can you see the reason why you must relax in times of trouble? Jesus is aware of your problem; HE will not leave you without a solution. HE is aware of your sickness; HE will not leave you without healing you. HE is aware of your poverty; HE will not leave you without blessings. When you are doing the right thing and are persecuted, Jesus is aware. Jesus is aware of your complaints; HE is aware of your yoke. HE will not leave you without freedom. As Jesus is aware of injustice, HE will not leave you without justice.

Therefore, be happy because Jesus is aware of every trial and every insult you receive from people as well as every problem, every difficulty and every crisis you face for righteousness' sake.

PRAYER POINTS

Jesus is aware of your problem;
HE will not leave you without solution.

Jesus is aware of your sickness;
HE will not leave you without healing.

Jesus is aware of your poverty;
HE will not leave you without blessings.

Say, "I am full of joy. I am happy because You, Jesus, are aware of every trial, insult, hardship and difficulty I face, in Your holy name."

STUDY QUESTIONS

ONE// Today, with your numerous copies of the Bible, numerous churches, countless pastors, crusades and seminars that you have access to, can you say that your faith in God is as strong as that of Job's?

TWO// Did God reveal to Job the trial he was about to face?

THREE// Today when many Christians are in a time of trial, they begin to query God, complaining that they have done so much for Him. As an upright man, why did Job not feel cheated by God in his severe trial?

FOR FURTHER READING

JAMES 1:2-4

JOB 19:25

JOB 23:10

JEREMIAH 17:5-8

ISAIAH 50:10

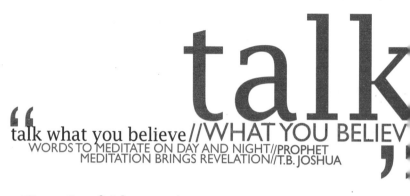

"By acting faith, satan's // JOB 1:6-22
mandate will
be destroyed."

"Christ's standard of // JOB 1:21
belief sees beyond
blessing."

"**Faith cannot take a** // COLOSSIANS 1:23
day off."

"Resist satan, the // JAMES 4:7-8
oppressor, staying
steadfastly in faith,
and claim your healing,
blessing and victory."

The Lord promised // MARK 10:29-30
to give you position,
money, prosperity and
authority, along with
persecution. If you
receive them by faith,
HE promised to see you
through.

"A confidence born of // JOB 31:24-28
faith depends wholly on
God for everything."

"We live by faith when // 2 CORINTHIANS 4:16-18
we recognise our union
with Jesus Christ in
the Spirit. Whereas we
live by sight when we
pay attention to the
physical body, which is
temporary."

daniel

Daniel's trial did not make him lose faith in God, rather it made him pray the more. DANIEL 6:1-28

"Now when Daniel learned that the decree had been published, he went home to his upstairs room where the windows opened toward Jerusalem. Three times a day he got down on his knees and prayed, giving thanks to his God, just as he had done before." DANIEL 6:10

When the decree was published, Daniel still went to the upper room and prayed louder than before. Can you see his faith? Daniel was a man of prayer; that was why they made the decree. The law of the Medes and Persians said that if anyone was caught praying in the name of the

DANIEL

God of Israel, he or she would be killed. That is the kind of faith we are talking about. Why was Daniel still praying? He knew his God was the God that saves and rescues.

Before you can show your faith, you must know your God as One that saves and rescues; you must know what you need Him to be. Before you can have faith in your God, you must first believe in Him alone and then trust in Him alone. You don't need to support God to do His work. Our duty is to have faith in His finished works. We try to support God when we combine Him with other gods. If Daniel had bowed down before another god, which would they have accepted as a state God? Which God would have taken the glory?

Daniel's experience of hard times was to be in the lion's den. The Bible says he had a look of faith at his situation as he was being led into the lion's den, and saw redemption and freedom. Such is a man of faith. He looked beyond his immediate situation unto redemption and freedom. He had no wound on him and felt no pain because of his belief. He believed in God and was saved from the plots of his adversary.

We should trust in God in every trial. In the hour of adversity, we should trust in God. For the reason that Daniel trusted in God in his hour of adversity, **his God became known all over, all the earth trembled before his God and his God was known as the God who rescues and delivers.**

When will you show your belief? Today, Christians believe in God but not in the times of trial.

They believe only when everything is going fine, when everyone is speaking well of them. When you are afraid, your god will be a god of fear. When you are in doubt during your crisis, your god will be a god of doubts. However, when you believe in God in your crisis, your God will be the God that rescues.

For the fact that he believed in God, Daniel was stronger than he was before he went into his crisis. What made him stronger?

ONE// His status was elevated.
TWO// He began to dine with kings and men of

substance: King Darius began to recognise him.

THREE// His faith became a state one: the whole country said, "The God of Daniel, everybody should worship, obey and respect!" A "state one" means the God that everyone believes in.

FOUR// His relationship with God shifted to another level.

PRAYER POINTS

Daniel was conscious of his faith even under pressure and tension.

Ask God to give you the grace to be conscious of your faith even under pressure and tension, in the mighty name of our Lord and Saviour, Jesus Christ.

Are you ready for prayer? We shall call the God of Daniel, the God that delivers at the point of need. Daniel needed God and the Lord rescued him. We shall call the God of Daniel to answer us by fire. God of Daniel! HE is the God that delivers at the point of need! Continue to call the God of Daniel, in

Jesus' name.

Be thou delivered, in the mighty name of Jesus Christ. Amen.

Thou power of deliverance, fall upon you, in Jesus' name! Fall upon your spirit, soul and body, in the mighty name of Jesus Christ! Thou power of freedom, fall upon you!

Jesus is now fighting for you as HE fought for Daniel in the lion's den. HE is now fighting for you as HE fought for Shadrach, Meshach and Abednego in the furnace.

Ask Him to fight for you. Say to Him, "Fight for me now, Lord, in Your holy name!"

God gave victory to Daniel in the lion's den.

"Oh Lord, by Your name, Jehovah Nissi, give me victory, in Your holy name!"

STUDY QUESTIONS

ONE// What kind of prayer would Daniel have offered when the decree was published? Would Daniel have prayed for more tension and pressure in worshipping his God?

TWO// Why did Daniel open his window and pray in the direction of Jerusalem? Was there any spiritual significance in doing so?

THREE// Who was in the lion's den before Daniel?

FOUR// When the lions could not devour Daniel, why could the government officials not try another method of killing him, since their aim was to kill him at all costs?

FOR FURTHER READING

ROMANS 8:31

PSALM 31:15

PHILIPPIANS 4:6

DEUTERONOMY 10:21

HEBREWS 11:33

2 TIMOTHY 4:18

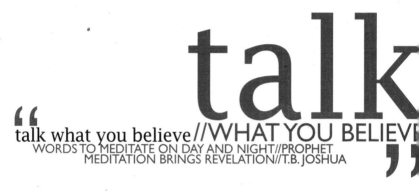

talk what you believe //WHAT YOU BELIEVE

WORDS TO MEDITATE ON DAY AND NIGHT//PROPHET
MEDITATION BRINGS REVELATION//T.B. JOSHUA

"A man of faith is led by // DANIEL 5:14-15
an indwelling Spirit of
grace, which is greater
than he who dwells in
the world."

"Before you can show // DANIEL 6:26-27
your faith, you must
know that your God is
the God that saves
and rescues."

"Trust in Jesus Christ // JOHN 11:26
and you will never be
confounded in
time or eternity."

"The moment you step into faith and stay there, satan cannot touch you."   // DANIEL 6:22

"You can never be promoted until your belief is tested. You can never be known until your belief is tested."   // DANIEL 6:26-28

"Don't murmur and rebel in your hour of adversity. Trust in God in every trial."   // PHILIPPIANS 2:14

peter

Jesus spoke the Word of assurance and Peter believed and took Jesus at His Word.

LUKE 5:4-8
MATTHEW 14:28-31
ACTS 3:1-8

"When he had finished speaking, he said to Simon, 'Put out into deep water, and let down the nets for a catch.' Simon answered, 'Master, we've worked hard all night and haven't caught anything. But because you say so, I will let down the nets.'

When they had done so, they caught such a large number of fish that their nets began to break. So they signalled their partners in the other boat to come and help them, and they came and filled both boats so full that they began to sink. When Simon Peter saw this, he fell at Jesus' knees and said, 'Go away from me, Lord; I am a sinful man!' " LUKE 5:4–8

The way Peter complained after struggling throughout the day and night showed that he was a poor man. He said, "Lord, if You say so..." - that is a poor man's way of talking. Peter was a man with limited means of survival. He was indeed very poor. What was the instruction given to him? "Simon, put down the nets for a catch." That was the instruction from Jesus.

The expression, "for a catch" shows the certainty and assurance of Jesus. The word, "certainty," means that Jesus was not guessing at all. HE was sure of what HE was saying. HE knew HE would not fail. Today, when the man of God says, "In the name of Jesus, be blessed", it is an assurance that God can bless through him. When the man of God says, "In the name of Jesus, be healed", it is an assurance that God can heal through him.

In this case, Jesus spoke the Word of assurance and Peter believed and took Jesus at His Word. If the man of God says, "Be blessed in Jesus' name", would you believe it would be done? That is the question now. It is not just all up to the man of God - you have a role to play. Your belief, your faith, also counts. It was not just all up to Jesus. When Jesus said to him, "Put down the nets for a catch", as a free moral agent, Peter had the right to say, "Thank You; I don't want to do that. I'm not interested; after all, I have toiled all night without a catch".

" 'Lord, if it's you,' Peter replied, 'tell me to come to you on the water.' 'Come,' he said. Then Peter got down out of the boat, walked on the water and came towards Jesus. But when he saw the wind, he was afraid and, beginning to sink, cried out, 'Lord, save me!' Immediately Jesus reached out his hand and caught him. 'You of little faith,' he said, 'why did you doubt?' " MATTHEW 14:28-31

Your obedience is the only proof of your faith in Him. Peter did what he had never done before. You can say you have faith, but without your obedience (faith in action) there is no proof. What is the meaning of the word, "faith"? The meaning is obedience. Christians must have faith in Christ Jesus because a Christian's life comes from Christ Himself. The reward for obedience will show if we truly have faith in Jesus. What is the reward for obedience? What is the reward for faith in your Master? The reward is when you are able to do what HE is doing. Jesus said: "I tell you the truth, anyone who has faith in me will do what I have been doing. He will do even greater things than these, because I am going to the Father." JOHN 14:12

Peter had the genuine desire to do the impossible, to reach the unreachable, so he cried out to Jesus. Jesus saw his faith and said, "Come!" Peter showed his faith as someone who wanted to come to Jesus. Jesus was on the sea. When HE saw Peter's faith, HE said, "Come!" HE did not see only Peter, HE saw Peter's faith. It is one thing to see you but it is another thing to see your faith. Jesus can see you without faith but you will not be blessed. HE will not bless you without faith. HE will not protect you without faith.

"Then Peter said, 'Silver or gold I do not have, but what I have I give you. In the name of Jesus Christ of Nazareth, walk'." **ACTS 3:6**

What Peter possessed was what he gave out: "In the name of Jesus Christ of Nazareth, walk." No one can say, "In the name of Jesus Christ" or "Jesus is Lord" without the help of the Holy Spirit. What Peter possessed was the Holy Spirit. Remember, the Bible says **when we accept Jesus as our Lord and personal Saviour, we have the very presence of God in our hearts through the Holy Spirit**. The Holy Spirit is another Comforter. Jesus was the first Comforter. In the absence of Jesus Christ, the Holy Spirit was to be sent (see **JOHN 14:16-18**).

So, what we need in our lives is the Holy Spirit to make us effective for Christ Jesus. What Peter possessed was the name, Jesus Christ, through the Holy Spirit. One can possess the name, Jesus Christ, through the Holy Spirit and give out the name, Jesus Christ, through the same Holy Spirit. Peter believed in Jesus and possessed Jesus Christ through the Holy Spirit. When you possess Him (Jesus Christ), you will do things through Him.

"Whoever believes in me, as the Scripture has said, streams of living water will flow from within him." JOHN 7:38

"Within him" means innermost being (i.e., heart). Christ Jesus describes the Holy Spirit as rivers of living water that flow out of the believer's innermost being. Peter believed in Jesus and possessed Him. How do we possess Jesus? **We possess Jesus Christ when we possess His character because God's Word reflects His character.** Your word reflects your character. If you are a thief, your characteristics are killing, stealing and destruction. What are the characteristics of Jesus? The characteristics of Jesus are the characteristics of the Holy Spirit (see GALATIANS 5:22-23).

The Bible refers to satan as the father of lies – the thief of our comfort and blessing, the killer and the destroyer of life. If you tell lies, you are speaking your father's language, for satan is the father of lies (see JOHN 8:44). If you kill, you are doing your father's job, for satan is a killer: he is the author of killing.

His diseases are the destroyers of life. His sicknesses are the thieves of happiness, health, money, time and effort. If you steal, you are doing your father's job, for satan is the thief of joy, peace and comfort. If you destroy, you are doing your father's job, for satan is a destroyer. The thief comes simply to kill, steal and destroy (see JOHN 10:10).

PRAYER POINTS

Peter wanted to come to Jesus. Jesus saw Peter's faith as someone who wanted to come to Him and Jesus told him to "Come!"

I want you to show your faith right now.
Show your faith!

The Lord wants to see your desire to get free, to get saved and to be blessed. Jesus saw Peter's desire to come to Him on the water and HE said to him, "Come!"

Say, "Lord Jesus, give me the grace to have a genuine desire, in Your holy name."

When Peter said, "Walk", he spoke life.

Right now, ask Jesus, our Saviour, to start speaking life unto your life and unto everything that has to do with you, in His name!

God sometimes uses foolish things to preserve us.

Ask God to use whatever situation you are in to preserve you, in Jesus' name.

STUDY QUESTIONS

ONE// What motivated Peter to say, "Go away from me, Lord, I am a sinful man"?

TWO// How did Peter manage the affairs of his family? What does the Bible say about his family?

THREE// How can we know that we are saved?

FOUR// How can we pray in the name of Jesus Christ and have results as Peter did?

FOR FURTHER READING
JOHN 4:50
I JOHN 3:22
ISAIAH 1:19
ACTS 5:29

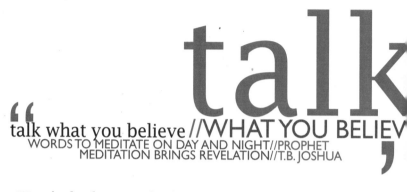

"talk what you believe // WHAT YOU BELIEV
WORDS TO MEDITATE ON DAY AND NIGHT//PROPHET
MEDITATION BRINGS REVELATION//T.B. JOSHUA

"Don't doubt your faith; // MATTHEW 14:31
doubt your doubts for
they are unreliable."

"Faith will make // ACTS 3:16
you operate in the
dimension in which God
operates."

"Just step into faith and // JOHN 11:40
see what will happen."

"We that love Jesus Christ // 2 CORINTHIANS 5:7
are walking by faith."

"Peter was convinced // LUKE 5:8-10
that Jesus Christ said
what HE meant and
meant what HE said."

"What you are able // MATTHEW 17:20
to do in the name of
Jesus depends on your
capacity to believe."

"When a person steps // MATTHEW 7:24
out in God's kind of
faith, he will be standing
on solid rock."

four-men

MARK 2:2-12

Faith can make the impossible possible.

"So many gathered that there was no room left, not even outside the door, and he preached the word to them. Some men came, bringing to him a paralytic, carried by four of them. Since they could not get him to Jesus because of the crowd, they made an opening in the roof above Jesus and, after digging through it, lowered the mat the paralysed man was lying on. When Jesus saw their faith, he said to the paralytic, 'Son, your sins are forgiven'. "
MARK 2:2-5

Jesus can notice you by faith. Jesus can see you by faith. Jesus can recognise you by faith. You can be attended to, recognised, noticed and appreciated by faith. When Jesus saw their faith, HE blessed and healed him.

ONE// Four men's faith enabled them
to reach the unreachable.
TWO// Four men's faith did what
no man had ever done.
THREE// Four men's faith achieved what
no man had ever achieved.
FOUR// Four men's faith made
the impossible possible.
FIVE// Four men's faith made a way
where there was no way.

Faith can make a way where there seems to be no way. Faith can make streams through dry valleys. Thus, faith can make the impossible possible.

Four men could not get to Jesus, but their faith could - through the valley of the shadow of death; through the impossible and through the unreachable. With faith, all things are possible. There was a barrier. The barrier here was the crowd but with faith, they reached Jesus by lowering the crippled man through the roof.

Jesus wants to see you do what no one has ever done. HE wants to see you make a way where there seems to be no way. HE wants to see you do what the ordinary man cannot. What is impossible for man, Jesus wants to see you do by faith. HE wants you to show your faith. Jesus saw Peter's faith and made him walk on water by giving a simple command for Peter to do what he had never done before (see MATTHEW 14:29). HE said, "Come", and when Peter had come out of the boat, he walked on the water to go to Jesus. **Our obedience is the only proof of our faith in Him.**

PRAYER POINTS

Position yourself for victory.

Lord Jesus, put me in a position that will attract Your attention and commitment, in Your holy name!

Lord Jesus, put me in a position where You will be interested in whatever I say and whatever I do, in Your holy name.

STUDY QUESTIONS

ONE// What was the reaction of the crowd and the owner of the house to the unusual act of the four men? What would the government of that day say about it since the house did not belong to them?

TWO// In a world overcrowded with people in need, what can you do to be noticed by the Saviour?

THREE// Why did Jesus see it necessary to say, "Go, your sins are forgiven", instead of saying, "Be healed" (See MARK 2:5)?

FOR FURTHER READING

JAMES 2:17-18

2 CHRONICLES 7:14

MATTHEW 17:20-21

JAMES 5:15-16

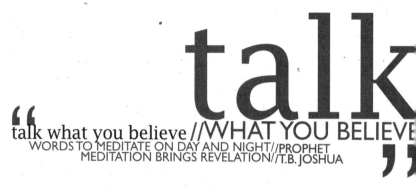

"talk what you believe //WHAT YOU BELIEVE
WORDS TO MEDITATE ON DAY AND NIGHT//PROPHET
MEDITATION BRINGS REVELATION//T.B. JOSHUA"

"Faith is the route   // ROMANS 5:1
to Jesus."

"The unreachable can be   // MARK 2:3-5
reached by faith."

"When you approach a   // MATTHEW 19:26
situation by faith, there
is no limit to what you
can achieve."

"Those possessing   // HEBREWS 11:32-37
this charisma or gift
called faith are able
to accomplish things
that are otherwise
impossible."

The Man At The
Pool Of Bethesda
JOHN 5:1-15

the man at the pool of bethesda

Believing in Christ Jesus redeems our time.

JOHN 5:1-15

"Here a great number of disabled people used to lie — the blind, the lame, the paralysed. One who was there had been an invalid for thirty-eight years. When Jesus saw him lying there and learned that he had been in this condition for a long time, he asked him, 'Do you want to get well?' 'Sir,' the invalid replied, 'I have no one to help me into the pool when the water is stirred. While I am trying to get in, someone else goes down ahead of me.' Then Jesus said to him, 'Get up! Pick up your mat and walk.'

93

At once the man was cured; he picked up his mat and walked...." JOHN 5:3-9

The man at the pool of Bethesda was there helpless for many years. Imagine a crippled man, struggling to enter the pool for many years. Imagine the hazards of the weather conditions. Remember, when it was raining or sunny, he was there.

When it was raining, it was extremely cold. When it was sunny, it was extremely hot and he was always there. He waited for God's appointed time. At God's appointed time, he was healed without any personal effort. **You will be healed today. You will be free today. You will be delivered today, without any personal effort.**

When he was looking for someone to carry him inside the pool, no one appeared. The Bible says, each time the angel of God stirred the waters, other people jumped into the pool. The crippled man was there, helplessly looking, listening to the testimonies of other people. He was not discouraged.

If this man had looked on the outside, he could have considered many things. What about all the healing he had seen? What about the other people who stepped into the water before him? What about those who were healed but had not been there as long as he had been? He could have said: "I'm going to the native doctor!" He could have given up. He had nobody to help him into the pool but that was looking on the outside. When you look on the outside of your situation, it becomes bigger than what you can handle, leading to fear, worry and anxiety.

If he was influenced by the happenings around, he would have given up. However, he maintained his calm for many years – under rainfall, sunshine, cold nights, mosquito bites, etc. Can someone who runs after Jesus for selfish reasons keep pressing under these kinds of conditions? The answer is NO! He kept pressing because he saw beyond his travails.

He believed that if only he could dip himself into the pool, he would be made whole. While waiting by the side of the pool, the Bible says, he heard many testimonies. Many others were healed in his presence. He was there lying with no one to help him but he was not discouraged. He saw many miracles happen to many others but there was one thing he believed in – God's time.

PRAYER POINTS

Today is your encounter with Jesus. Jesus is on His way to you – HE is coming purposely for you. HE is only a moment away.

Say, "Lord Jesus Christ, let Your mighty power be released into my body today, in Your holy name!"

STUDY QUESTIONS

ONE// There were other lame and paralysed people there that had received their healing. Why did this particular man spend 38 years beside the pool of Bethesda?

TWO// Jesus could obviously see that the man was in a miserable state. Why then did HE ask him, "Do you want to get well?"

THREE// What did Jesus mean when HE said, "...'See, you have been made well. Sin no more, lest a worse thing come upon you' "?

FOR FURTHER READING
ISAIAH 40:31
JAMES 5:7
PSALM 27:13-14
JOHN 16:21-22
ECCLESIASTES 11:1
ECCLESIASTES 3:1-11

" talk what you believe //WHAT YOU BELIEVE
WORDS TO MEDITATE ON DAY AND NIGHT//PROPHET
MEDITATION BRINGS REVELATION//T.B. JOSHUA "

"For your blessing to   // JOHN 5:14
stand the test of time,
your belief needs to
look beyond the
blessing you receive."

"When you stay in faith   //ACTS 26:18
in Christ Jesus, you can
stay far from sin."

"We accept a miracle by   //JOHN 9:35-38
faith when we
recognise the reason
for the miracle."

"There is no way you // GALATIANS 3:14
can maintain the
blessing of God
without faith."

"Are you in any // PSALM 37:7
unpleasant situation?
Wait patiently for the
Lord. Don't be worried
about your situation.
God's time is the best."

"Don't be anxious for // MATTHEW 6:25-34
anything – for they will
come when the time
comes."

the centurion

MATTHEW 8:5-13

The Centurion acknowledged his position as a sinner in need of salvation.

"Now when Jesus had entered Capernaum, a centurion came to Him, pleading with Him, saying, 'Lord, my servant is lying at home paralysed, dreadfully tormented.' And Jesus said to him, 'I will come and heal him.' The centurion answered and said, 'Lord, I am not worthy that You should come under my roof. But only speak a word, and my servant will be healed. For I also am a man under·authority, having soldiers under me. And I say to this one, 'Go,' and he goes; and to another, 'Come,' and he comes; and to my servant, 'Do this,' and he does it.' When Jesus heard it, He marvelled, and said to those who followed, 'Assuredly, I say to you, I have not found such great faith, not even in Israel!' " MATTHEW 8:5-10 NKJV

When we come to God in any form, HE sees beyond our appearance. If a man speaks, Jesus knows whether his intent is merely to flatter or to speak what he truly believes in his heart. We know what men do but Jesus knows the designs of their hearts. In the case of the Centurion, Jesus did not base His judgment on the Centurion's open confession of His Lordship over all earthly authorities but on the disposition of his heart.

To honour God is to acknowledge our position as one undeserving of His presence. To acknowledge our position is to admit our weakness, our shortcoming, before Him. The Centurion was the leader of a battalion of soldiers, a war general. Yet he acknowledged his position before our Lord Jesus Christ when he said, "...'Lord, I am not worthy that You should come under my roof...'. " MATTHEW 8:8 NKJV He acknowledged his position as a sinner in need of salvation. How do we acknowledge our position? We do so by coming unto

God in humility and sincerity of heart.

Let us see how Jesus feels when we come in sincerity and humility of mind, when we admit our position, when we admit our weakness and when we acknowledge our position as sinners.

"When Jesus heard it, He marvelled, and said to those who followed, 'Assuredly, I say to you, I have not found such great faith, not even in Israel!' " MATTHEW 8:10 NKJV

HE marvelled. When you admit your weakness in sincerity and humility of mind, not just on the outside but on the inside, Jesus does not only marvel, HE is also happy to receive you with compassion.

Jesus Christ has authority over the devil and his agents that steal, kill and destroy. The Centurion was telling Jesus, "I am a man of authority on the outside, but You are a man of authority on the inside. Greater is HE that is with us than he that is on the outside, so I submit." Why did the Centurion come to Jesus? He came to Jesus because he was looking for Him that had all authority over the devil. His physical instruments of war as a general had failed and he said: "I know You have the authority to tell this sickness to go, and it will go."

Jesus told him to go home and his servant was healed that hour. This demonstrates the power in the spoken word:

" '...But only speak a word, and my servant will be healed'. "
MATTHEW 8:8 NKJV

The Bible says, HE sent forth His Word and healed them, saved them, delivered them and set them free (see PSALM 107:20). The Centurion knew this. That was why he asked Jesus to speak a Word and his servant was healed indeed.

"Then Jesus said to the centurion, 'Go your way; and as you have believed, so let it be done for you.' And his servant was healed that same hour." MATTHEW 8:13 NKJV

The authority of Jesus is not limited by space and time. Distance is not a barrier to the authority of our Lord and our Saviour; time is not a barrier; worldly authority is not a barrier. The only thing that limits His authority is our belief.

His Words are made health to all flesh. Remember the Centurion who received a Word and his servant was healed.

PRAYER POINTS

Let us pray: Lord, our soul is waiting for You. In Your Word is our hope. In Your Word is our healing. In Your Word is our blessing. In Your Word is our salvation, in Your holy name.

I pray today for miracles; let Your Word bring them - healing, blessing and salvation. I rebuke that sickness, that unpleasant situation. I give You praise, in Your holy name.

When the Holy Spirit speaks, changes are beginning.

Ask God to give you a Word that will change the course of your life forever, in Jesus' name.

If you realise that the level of your faith is not enough to receive from Jesus, remember: you are not called upon to look within yourself to see how much faith you have but you are called upon to look to Jesus and take from Him the faith HE has prepared to give you.

"Lord Jesus, add to my faith, in Your holy name! Give me Your kind of faith. Make me to believe in Your own way, in Your mighty name."

STUDY QUESTIONS

ONE// Why did Jesus say the Centurion's faith was greater, "even than that of anyone in Israel"?

TWO// What was it that convinced the Centurion that just a Word from Jesus was enough to change the course of his servant's life, who was far away?

THREE// What does it mean to come before God in sincerity and humility of mind as the Centurion did?

FOR FURTHER READING
LUKE 7:1-10
MATTHEW 28:18
PSALM 145:18-19
ISAIAH 55:11
PSALM 130:5-6

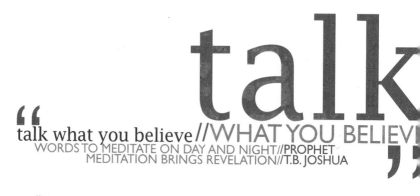

"talk what you believe //WHAT YOU BELIEV
WORDS TO MEDITATE ON DAY AND NIGHT//PROPHET
MEDITATION BRINGS REVELATION//T.B. JOSHUA"

"Every time you speak // MATTHEW 8:5-13
the Words of Faith, you
hear yourself and God
hears you. But every
time you do not speak
the Words of Faith, you
only hear yourself; God
does not hear you."

"Whatever is possible // MARK 9:23
for you depends on your
level of belief."

"If you believe in // JEREMIAH 17:7
something, you should
have confidence in
that thing."

"Jesus Christ believes what you and I say is important." // MATTHEW 12:36-37

"Jesus' authority is not limited by space and time; this means distance is not a barrier. It is only your belief that limits His authority." // JOHN 4:49-53

"True faith or divine faith, when expressed in prayer, is a force that has God behind it for its accomplishment." // ISAIAH 55:11

"If you believe God's Word is true for your life, you can begin to claim His promises by confessing them now." // 2 CORINTHIANS 1:20

the prostitute

LUKE 7:37-50

From the moment Jesus entered her life, HE put an end to her life of prostitution.

"And behold, a woman in the city who was a sinner, when she knew that Jesus sat at the table in the Pharisee's house, brought an alabaster flask of fragrant oil, and stood at His feet behind Him weeping; and she began to wash His feet with her tears, and wiped them with the hair of her head; and she kissed His feet and anointed them with the fragrant oil. Now when the Pharisee who had invited Him saw this, he spoke to himself, saying, 'This Man, if He were a prophet, would know who and what manner of woman this is who is touching Him, for she is a sinner'. " LUKE 7:37-39 NKJV

The Pharisee saw the woman in the past and in the present; he did not consider her future. He saw her as a sinful woman and felt the woman would not have anything to do with Jesus at present. That was his judgment. He judged her past and any other woman in her position, who is without vision, would feel condemned because of her sin. The prostitute was not looking at where she was coming from but where she was going. She was a woman of vision. This is to show that when you have a vision, nothing can stop you from reaching your goal. No hardship, trouble, sickness, or even unrighteousness can stop you from reaching your goal.

When you are a man of vision, you will not look at where you are coming from but where you are going. For her to run after Jesus as a prostitute, she must have had a vision which said: "If only I can reach Jesus, I will be made whole," and she was made whole indeed. Your vision has to do with where you are going, not where you are coming from. You are coming from sin and going to Jesus. Faith is moving towards the direction of Jesus. Faith is the cause of victory; it is the means, the instrument and the spiritual armour by which we overcome sin and the world.

The Bible says, **when Jesus enters our lives, HE ends our past and gives birth to our future**. This woman had a vision and that was why she was running after Jesus. What was her vision? Her vision said: "If only I can reach Jesus, I know I will be clean, I will be healed of my sin." When you are healed of sin, you are healed indeed.

Whatever situation you are in, the way you handle it matters. Remember, the whole world is watching you; among them your friends and foes.

Prostitutes, we know, run after their "customers" - those who patronise them, but here was a prostitute running after a holy man. Certainly, she must have had a vision known to her alone. What is your situation? Whatever your situation, the way you handle it matters. That she was a prostitute does not mean she did not have a vision. The prostitute was bold enough to run after Jesus because she had a vision that if only she could reach Jesus, it would be well and the Bible says it was well with her indeed. The Bible says when you have a vision, it will give you courage, confidence and boldness to go on – no matter what anyone says, no matter what happens and no matter your circumstance. **A vision imparts into you the strength to endure your present tribulation.**

Remember, Jesus saw the woman's faith as someone who wanted to come to Him. How do we show our faith? We show our faith when we start looking at where we are going instead of where we are coming from. Remember, you are coming from sin – unfaithfulness, hatred, lying, impatience, etc. This woman was coming from sin. Jesus said: "Therefore, I say unto you, your many sins are forgiven, because you loved so much."

Many run after Jesus without vision. Such people can be stopped by circumstances: sickness, poverty, fear, doubt, etc. Circumstances can make them change their confession easily. They move around churches and men of God, not around Jesus, because they have no vision.

PRAYER POINTS

From the moment Jesus entered her life, HE put an end to her life of prostitution. HE said to her: "Your many sins are forgiven." She believed if she could meet or touch Jesus, she would be made whole.

When you look at the case of the prostitute, you will realise that Jesus did not look at where she was coming from. From the moment Jesus entered her life, HE put an end to her life of prostitution. We know that the life of a prostitute is that of lust, impurity and anger - all of the fruits of the flesh.

Ask Jesus to come into your life and put an end to your bad habits! It was bad habits that made her a prostitute.

Say, "Lord Jesus, put an end to my bad habits - lust, envy, jealousy, impurity, immorality and anger, in Your holy name."

This means Jesus enters our life to put an end to where we are coming from and give birth to where we are going.

"Therefore I say to you, her sins, which are many, are forgiven." LUKE 7:47

Your "sins which are many," are what the Bible refers to here.

Right now, Lord Jesus, we ask You to speak forgiveness into our lives. Speak forgiveness into our lives, in Your mighty name.

Jesus never disconnected Himself from those who made mistakes with their lives. What are your mistakes? They are correctable. What have you done wrong? Remember the prostitute. Jesus said to her, "Therefore I say to you, your many sins are forgiven."

Therefore, I say unto you, your many sins are forgiven, in Jesus' name.

STUDY QUESTION

ONE// Considering her position in society, what gave the prostitute the boldness to enter a religious leader's house?

FOR FURTHER READING
ISAIAH 43:18-19
PSALM 73:21-24
COLOSSIANS 1:13-14
ROMANS 3:22-24
ISAIAH 1:18
ISAIAH 55:7

talk what you believe//WHAT YOU BELIEVE

WORDS TO MEDITATE ON DAY AND NIGHT//PROPHET
MEDITATION BRINGS REVELATION//T.B. JOSHUA

"By an act of faith, you // PHILIPPIANS 3:12-14
begin to think not of
your sins and
shortcomings
but of your
righteousness in
Christ Jesus."

"Faith justifies and // ROMANS 5:1-2
purifies us, and thus
removes the mountain
of guilt that had
separated us from God."

"It is only by believing // GALATIANS 3:6
that we are made right."

"How does // ACTS 15:9
faith overcome
sin and the world?
Faith sanctifies
the heart and purifies it
from those lusts
of the world."

"Show your faith as // MARK 10:46-52
someone who wants to
come to Jesus."

"The Bible says Jesus // I SAMUEL 17:45
shows Himself strong on
behalf of those who
depend on Him."

"When you // LUKE 22:49-52
believe in Jesus,
beyond your mistake,
there's correction."

The Woman With The Issue Of Blood
MARK 5:25-34

the woman with the issue of blood

MARK 5:25-34

What you receive from God comes as a result of you actively reaching out and claiming God's promises.

"Now a certain woman had a flow of blood for twelve years, and had suffered many things from many physicians. She had spent all that she had and was no better, but rather grew worse. When she heard about Jesus, she came behind Him in the crowd and touched His garment. For she said, 'If only I may touch His clothes, I shall be made well'. "

MARK 5:25-28 NKJV

The woman with the issue of blood touched the hem of Jesus' garment. She was not the only person to touch the hem of His garment. Hers was a touch born of faith. She touched the hem of His garment to attract the attention of Jesus, not the attention of men. She was not there to tempt Jesus.

Certainly, she had a vision known to her alone, for she said: "If only I may touch His clothes, I shall be made well", and she was well indeed.

What is your vision? My vision says: "If I can reach Jesus, I shall be well. If I can obey His Word, I shall be well."

PRAYER POINTS

Jesus is as close to you as HE was to the woman with the issue of blood. The woman with the issue of blood wanted to come to Jesus and, also, showed her faith. Right now, show your faith; show your belief. If your faith is not enough, you should ask Him for more.

If your faith is not enough, right now, in the mighty name of Jesus Christ, receive!

You are not asked to look within and see how much faith you have. You are asked to look to Jesus. Look to Jesus by His Word.

Your capacity to believe in Jesus as the Healer, as the Saviour - begin to increase in His holy name!

Lord Jesus, increase their capacity to believe! In Your powerful name.

STUDY QUESTIONS

ONE// The Bible says in MARK 5:30, "At once, Jesus realised that power had gone out from him." When the woman touched the hem of His garment, what did she experience?

TWO// Being an outcast, what kind of opposition do you think this woman faced on her way to reach Jesus?

THREE// Are you seeking Jesus because of your vision, or because you see others doing so?

FOUR// Since it had never been a practise to touch the hem of Jesus' garment in that way, what brought about the idea? Why did the woman not think Jesus would be offended when it had never been the practise before?

FOR FURTHER READING
LUKE 8:43-48
MATTHEW 9:29
LUKE 17:19
LUKE 18:42
HEBREWS 11:6

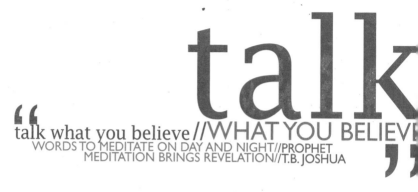

talk what you believe // WHAT YOU BELIEVE

WORDS TO MEDITATE ON DAY AND NIGHT//PROPHET
MEDITATION BRINGS REVELATION//T.B. JOSHUA

"Your faith is important;   // ISAIAH 1:19
I mean your genuine
willingness also
counts."

"You cannot possess   // HOSEA 6:3
what you are unwilling
to pursue."

"I believe - that is my   // ROMANS 10:6-10
connection."

"As faith focuses on // MARK 5:28
God, doubt focuses on
problems."

"Faith means our // MARK 5:25-27
movement towards
God."

The Canaanite Woman
MATTHEW 15:22-28

the canaa-nite woman

If the Canaanite woman had run after Jesus without faith, she would have been stopped.

"And behold, a woman of Canaan came from that region and cried out to Him, saying, 'Have mercy on me, O Lord, Son of David! My daughter is severely demon-possessed.' But He answered her not a word. And His disciples came and urged Him, saying, 'Send her away, for she cries out after us.' But He answered and said, 'I was not sent except to the lost sheep of the house of Israel.' Then she came and worshipped Him, saying, 'Lord, help me!' But He answered and said, 'It is not good to take the children's bread and throw it to the little dogs'. "
MATTHEW 15:22-26 NKJV

Jesus said, "I was sent only to the lost

sheep of Israel" and the woman was not an Israelite. Jesus ignored her. The term "dogs", as used in the Holy Bible, portrays someone without honour and respect. If the woman had no faith, the contempt she received would have been enough to discourage her. At first she was ignored and then she was humiliated by the disciples; she would have given up and surrendered. Indeed, she was running after Jesus by faith. How many of you can stand such a situation?

If the woman had run after Jesus without faith, she would have been stopped. She was a diligent seeker. A diligent seeker is one who believes in God in both good and hard times alike; one who is steadfast in his faith and one who sees his good times as a reason for believing in Jesus, just as he sees his hard times in the same way.

What lesson can we learn from this woman? Patience, perseverance, endurance, forbearance are the tools, the instruments, for a man of faith. A man without faith is a man without perseverance, forbearance, endurance and patience.

The Canaanite woman showed that she believed in the Person of Jesus. She never had any doubt at all; that was why she was crying. People of God, learn from this woman, the rewards of patience, perseverance and forbearance. Her patience, perseverance and forbearance surely produced many fruits.

Give God time and you will see the results working themselves out – slowly but surely. Your prayers and fasting are not lost. They will come back to you a hundredfold at God's own time.

The way this woman of Canaan was ignored at first was capable of discouraging her.

One should remember that man has the power of decision but the Holy Spirit decides as HE wills. While the woman of Canaan was talking to Jesus, there was conflict in her mind as to whether to continue or not. Thus, man has the ability to think of many things but the Holy Spirit has the power to decide as HE wills.

Put yourself in her position. How would you feel at that moment, with Jesus ignoring you and the disciples urging Him to drive you away? How would you feel? For a human being, this is a moment of conflict. A man without vision would have many things going through his mind: he would begin to see Jesus in a bad light, or, he would give up. As the Canaanite woman had faith and vision, she endured and continued to strive until she was answered.

PRAYER POINTS

The woman was ignored at first by Jesus, but she kept pressing because she had a vision. She kept pressing because she had the vision that if only she could reach Jesus, it would be well with her.

Don't give up! Keep pressing on in His own way, in His own name and in His own time. The Lord will send the harvest! Don't give up. Give God time! The results are working themselves out – slowly but surely! In the face of poverty or sickness, don't give up! HE will not leave you without blessing or healing.

God's kind of patience has no limits. Ask Him to give it to you, in Jesus' name.

If your patience has a limit, then it is man's patience. Suppose the woman's patience had limits; she would have given up along the line.

Right now, ask Jesus to give you patience, enough patience, in His name.

Ask Jesus to give you love, enough love, in His name.

Ask Jesus to give you perseverance, enough perseverance, in His name.

Ask Jesus to give you forbearance, enough forbearance, in His name.

Ask Jesus to give you endurance, enough endurance, in His name.

STUDY QUESTIONS

ONE// Why did Jesus not attend to the Canaanite woman immediately? What made Jesus ignore her at first?

TWO// "And she said, 'Yes, Lord, yet even the little dogs

eat the crumbs which fall from their masters' table.' "
MATTHEW 15:27 What did the woman mean
by 'crumbs?'

THREE// Nothing could change the mind of the
Canaanite woman concerning what she believed
about Jesus. Why did she remain persistent and not
take offence to Jesus' response?

FOR FURTHER READING

MARK 7:24-30

JAMES 1:6

PSALM 31:24

LUKE 18:1-8

JAMES 5:11

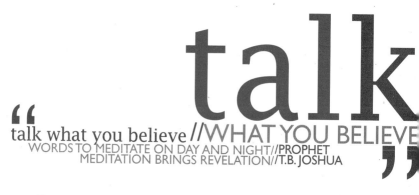

talk

"
talk what you believe //WHAT YOU BELIEVE
WORDS TO MEDITATE ON DAY AND NIGHT//PROPHET
MEDITATION BRINGS REVELATION//T.B. JOSHUA
"

"Your vision will give   //MATTHEW 15:22-28
you courage, confidence
and boldness to go on,
no matter what anyone
says, no matter what
happens and no matter
your circumstance."

"Faith fills our soul with   //LUKE 18:1-8
a strong desire
for the things we are
praying for."

"Faith is not a feeling."   //MATTHEW 16:22-23

"We are told to ask for // JAMES 1:5-6
wisdom, healing and
blessing, but let us
ask in faith -
nothing wavering."

"You must put yourself // ISAIAH 65:24
in a position where God // PSALM 40:1
will incline His ears
unto you, ready to listen
and where God would
commit Himself to what
you say and do in faith."

"If you believe Jesus // DANIEL 3:16-18
is the Deliverer, you
should have confidence
in His ability to deliver,
no matter what comes.
From this confidence
comes perseverance,
endurance and
patience."

The Father Of The Demon Possessed Boy
MARK 9:17-29

the father

of the demon-possessed boy

MARK 9:17-29

You are not called upon to look within to see how much faith you have but to look to God and take from Him the faith you need.

"Then one of the crowd answered and said, 'Teacher, I brought You my son, who has a mute spirit. And wherever it seizes him, it throws him down; he foams at the mouth, gnashes his teeth, and becomes rigid. So I spoke to Your disciples, that they should cast it out, but they could not.' He answered him and said, 'O faithless generation, how long shall I be with you? How long shall I bear with you? Bring him to Me'. " MARK 9:17-19 NKJV

Among the crowd the father of the demon-possessed boy was the only person that put to shame the faithless generation. He put the faithless generation to shame by stepping out and claiming God's promises. Who are the faithless generation? The crowd. Among them were the teachers of the law and the Pharisees. The Bible says the father of the demon-possessed boy stepped out and took Jesus at His Word. He stepped out by his belief in Christ Jesus. He stepped out by his prayer for help, saying: "...I believe; help my unbelief!" MARK 9:24 NKJV This statement is both a prayer for help and a declaration of his belief in Jesus.

Right now, I know many of us have been held back by our association with friends, religion, culture or traditional beliefs. Right now we want to step out. The father of the demon-possessed boy stepped out. From the crowd, he stepped out, saying: "I believe like my people, help me to believe in Your own way."

He stepped out of the crowd. Among this crowd were Pharisees and teachers of the law who had traditional beliefs. As you stand before your difficulty, you have to acknowledge your need. The difficulty of this man was the sick boy. The man had no faith in the ones Jesus had sent to act on His behalf; that was why Jesus lamented, saying: " 'O faithless generation, how long shall I be with you? How long shall I bear with you? Bring him to Me.' " MARK 9:19 NKJV

This man had no faith but he ran to Jesus. This teaches us that you should look to Jesus and take the faith you need from Him.

" '...But if You can do anything, have compassion on us and help us.' " MARK 9:22 NKJV

This shows a genuine desire on the part of the seeker. This kind of language shows hopelessness. It means, he had nothing. When you are a genuine seeker, you are not called upon to look within to see how much faith you have but to look to God and take from Him the faith you need. Look to His Word because God is in His Word.

When it comes to healing, Jesus never heals alone. HE demands people's faith. HE seeks for a genuine desire on the part of the seeker because healing is for salvation and for the glory of God.

One thing is clear, the seeker must show a genuine desire – a genuine willingness on his or her part. A genuine desire on the part of the seeker, plus God's ability in the life of His servant, brings healing and miracles.

Step out from faithless association! Remember, many things have been holding you back. Right now, it is time to step out from the association of friends and your culture. Step out, in Jesus Christ's name! Remember, the father of the demon-possessed boy met Jesus. Before his encounter with Jesus, he never saw anything wrong in his belief. Nevertheless, immediately he met Jesus, he realised his weakness. Have you realised your weakness? Begin to confess your weakness, limitation or shortcoming!

PRAYER POINTS

Today, I say unto you that you are going to put the

faithless generation to shame, in Jesus' name. I mean, today you shall put satan and all his vices around you to shame, in Jesus' name.

Remember, some people are watching you; among them are your friends and foes – those who are waiting to ask you, "Where is your God?" You shall put all of them to shame today, in Jesus' name.

Before the father of the demon-possessed boy met Jesus, he did not see anything wrong with the standard of his belief. Remember, his standard of belief was the same as those of other members of the crowd. That was why they had the same mind towards the disciples of Jesus. However, when he met Jesus, he understood the weakness of his belief and then stepped out with boldness, thereby renouncing his association with the faithless generation. Stepping out, he cried to Jesus: "I know I believe like my people – now I know I need to believe in Your own way."

I know many of us today have been held back by our own association with friends, relations, cultures and traditional beliefs. Now I say unto you: like the father of the demon-possessed boy, you shall step out with boldness today and take God at His Word, in Jesus' name.

Right now begin to step out and take God at His Word, in Jesus' name.

Remember, the father of the demon-possessed boy put the faithless generation to shame with his belief and prayer saying, " '...I believe; help my unbelief'. " MARK 9:24 NKJV This statement is both an expression of belief in our Lord Jesus Christ and a prayer for help.

Lord Jesus, I know I believe like my people but help me to believe in Your own way, in Your holy name.

STUDY QUESTIONS

ONE// When Jesus said, "Oh, unbelieving generation," who was HE referring to?

TWO// "So He said to them, 'This kind can come out by nothing but prayer and fasting.' " MARK 9:29 What did Jesus mean by 'this kind'? What kind of prayer and fasting was Jesus referring to?

THREE// When faced with a problem that refuses to yield to your prayer, how do you handle it?

FOUR// What made the demon-possessed boy to trigger when Jesus looked at him?

FOR FURTHER READING

MATTHEW 17:14-20

LUKE 9:38-43

ROMANS 3:3-4

MARK 11:22-24

MATTHEW 8:26

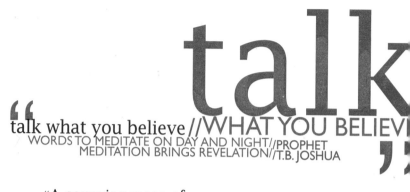

talk what you believe//WHAT YOU BELIEVE

WORDS TO MEDITATE ON DAY AND NIGHT//PROPHET
MEDITATION BRINGS REVELATION//T.B. JOSHUA

"A consciousness of // LUKE 17:5
little faith is far from
being a reason why we
should not ask. It should
be an encouragement,
an inspiration, and a
motivation."

"If one's faith must // JOHN 3:1-21
grow, it has to start in a
weak form."

"Jesus is disappointed // MARK 9:17-19
that men lack the
necessary faith to
release the power that
has been given them."

If you discover that // MARK 9:23-24
your ability to receive of
Jesus is hindered by the
level of your belief, you
can pray for it and Jesus
will be ready to make
you believe in
His own way.

"Those that complain of // MARK 9:19-25
unbelief, little faith or
no faith, must look up
to Christ and take the
faith HE is prepared
to give."

"Traditional belief is // MATTHEW 23:1-31
equal to unbelief before
Jesus Christ."

martha

Faith is expecting Jesus JOHN 11:1-44
to do what HE promised
to do.

Martha showed an absolute faith in Jesus, saying: " '...if You had been here, my brother [Lazarus] would not have died. But I know that even now [that he has died] God will give you whatever You ask.' " JOHN 11: 21-22

What a faith. This was the kind of faith Jesus needed to meet their needs. This is the kind of faith Jesus needs to meet your needs today – the faith, the genuine willingness of someone who wants to see Him.

149

Only Martha showed an absolute faith in Jesus Christ. She recognised Jesus as Saviour, Redeemer and Deliverer. She realised that belief in Jesus Christ is a prerequisite for the battle against satan. Belief is the condition. This was the kind of faith Jesus needed to meet their needs – the kind of faith HE needs to meet your needs today.

When we express the necessary trust in Jesus, His work is to raise us from death to life and then restore our wholeness and fellowship.

PRAYER POINTS

Lord Jesus, give us the kind of faith You need to meet our needs, in Your holy name.

Lord, let every doubt in my heart turn into faith. Let every unbelief in my heart turn into belief, in Your mighty name.

Open my heart to faith.
Open my heart to Your Spirit.
Open my heart to Your Words, in Your name.

STUDY QUESTIONS

ONE// The situation at the graveside of Lazarus ordinarily did not call for thanksgiving. When Lazarus was dead, in the grave, why did Jesus thank God (see JOHN 11:41-42)?

TWO// Why did Jesus cry when HE knew HE could raise Lazarus (see JOHN 11:35)?

FOR FURTHER READING

2 CORINTHIANS 5:7

JOHN 20:29

HEBREWS 11:1,35

PSALM 33:20-22

"talk what you believe // **WHAT YOU BELIEVE**
WORDS TO MEDITATE ON DAY AND NIGHT//**PROPHET**
MEDITATION BRINGS REVELATION//**T.B. JOSHUA**"

"A man of faith will say, // JOHN 11:41-42
'Thank You for bless-
ing me', even when the
signs of poverty are yet
there. A man of faith
will say, 'Thank You for
healing me', even when
the pain is still there.
This is an absolute faith;
this is an absolute trust
that HE is working out
the answer."

When we express the necessary faith in Jesus Christ, His duty is to raise us from death to life. I mean, when you express the necessary faith in Him, you discover a new goal and purpose.

// JOHN 11:25-44

"Faith focuses on God instead of your problems."

// JOHN 16:33

blind bartimaeus

MARK 10:46-52

As a Christian, when you have a vision, no amount of opposition or obstruction can change your mind.

"…As Jesus and his disciples, together with a large crowd, were leaving the city, a blind man, Bartimaeus (that is, the Son of Timaeus), was sitting by the roadside begging. When he heard that it was Jesus of Nazareth, he began to shout, 'Jesus, Son of David, have mercy on me!' Many rebuked him and told him to be quiet, but he shouted all the more, 'Son of David, have mercy on me!' Jesus stopped and said, 'Call him.' So they called to the blind man, 'Cheer up! On your feet! He's calling you'. "

MARK 10:46-49

Blind Bartimaeus shouted to be heard by Jesus, not by men. This was a shout born of faith which could not be stopped by any opposition. That was why the opposition could not stop him. That was why every attempt to stop him proved abortive. What an effort born of faith! What a genuine willingness born of faith! He was there to see Jesus: he was not there to be seen by men. Blind Bartimaeus shouted as someone who wanted to see Jesus. Anyone can shout. The Bible says he shouted as someone who wanted to see Jesus. I know many people will say: "I cry many times to receive Jesus' healing, but I don't get healed."

A shout born of God, Jesus never ignores. A shout born of God cannot but yield the desired results. A shout born of God cannot be stopped, no matter the degree of opposition. Bartimaeus' shout was born of faith: it was not just a shout.

"Many rebuked him and told him to be quiet, but he shouted all the more, 'Son of David, have mercy on me!' "
MARK 10:48

You can see how every attempt to stop the blind man

proved abortive – it was because the shout was born of faith. This is different from other shouts for selfish and material reasons, which can be stopped.

Bartimaeus had enough antagonism, enough opposition and enough obstruction to stop him. If you have a vision, nothing can stop you from reaching Jesus; nothing can prevent you from reaching your goal. Faith will fill your soul with a strong desire for the things you are praying for, even when the circumstance seems unfavourable.

For an example, where there is faith, there will be a strong desire to pray the more, even in the face of difficulties. Consider the case of Paul and Silas; the more they were flogged, the stronger their desire was to praise God.

PRAYER POINTS

Son of David, have mercy on me!
Let Your mercy speak for me today!

If today favours you, the rest of your life shall enjoy the divine favour of God.

By the power of God, I command today to favour you – let His mercy speak for you.

If Saul could receive divine favour and later became Paul, there is nothing impossible for Jesus.

Continue to receive divine favour in your business, career, home, family and marital life, in Jesus' name.

"Lord, let Your divine mercy favour me today, in Jesus' name."

Begin to command the closed doors to mercy, to open, in Jesus' name.

Begin to command the closed doors to favour, to open, in Jesus' name.

Begin to command the closed doors to breakthrough, to open, in Jesus' name.

STUDY QUESTIONS

ONE// What made blind Bartimaeus shout, "Have mercy on me", and not, "Heal me"?

TWO// Why did he follow Jesus along the road after receiving his sight?

THREE// What made blind Bartimaeus' shout attract Jesus, while others' did not?

FOUR// Many people come before Jesus, as His people come, but they only come to be seen by men, rather than Jesus. How do you come to Jesus?

FOR FURTHER READING
MATTHEW 20:29-34
LUKE 18:35-43
ISAIAH 55:3
PSALM 107:1-9, 28-29
PSALM 30:8-12

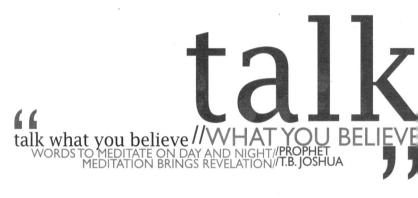

" talk what you believe // WHAT YOU BELIEVE
WORDS TO MEDITATE ON DAY AND NIGHT // PROPHET
MEDITATION BRINGS REVELATION // T.B. JOSHUA "

"You must exercise faith   // MARK 10:46-52
in Him, that is, act faith
in Him."

"Belief gives birth   // ROMANS 10:10
to confession."

"Faith in Christ Jesus is   // LUKE 8:50
a necessary condition
for true spiritual
healing, blessing and
salvation."

"Faith is in the // MARK 10:47-48
present tense. Faith
acts now, believes now,
receives now."

"You are not blessed for // LUKE 1:45
desiring to be blessed;
you are blessed because
you believe in
Christ Jesus."

Zacchaeus
LUKE 19:1-10

zacch-aeus

Without an attitude of repentance and faith, God's power cannot work in a man's heart.

LUKE 19:1-10

"Jesus entered Jericho and was passing through. A man was there by the name of Zacchaeus; he was a chief tax collector and was wealthy. He wanted to see who Jesus was, but being a short man he could not, because of the crowd. So he ran ahead and climbed a sycamore-fig tree to see him, since Jesus was coming that way. When Jesus reached the spot, he looked up and said to him, 'Zacchaeus, come down immediately. I must stay at your house today'. " LUKE 19:1-5

Zacchaeus was born a short

163

man. There was nothing he could do about it. We call it a natural circumstance of birth. However, the fact that he was a short man could not stop him from reaching his goal. His stature could not stop him because he had a vision: he wanted an encounter with Jesus.

"A man was there by the name of Zacchaeus; he was a chief tax collector and was wealthy." LUKE 19:2

This man wanted an encounter with Jesus. He was rich and lacked nothing. Though he was rich and lacked nothing in material terms, he was in need of redemption. It was funny to see a rich man climb a tree the way he did. Have you ever seen a rich man climb a tree? Ordinarily, no one would have expected a man like him to climb a tree. The Bible says that Zacchaeus was rich but he needed to see Jesus. He just needed an encounter with Jesus at all costs. So, if his height was going to disturb him, he was ready to disgrace satan. In desperation he had to climb the tree.

The Bible explains that there is a mixture of God's

grace and power with man's will and faith. I mean, the Word of God is to cause faith and the grace of God is to cover sins. Zacchaeus exercised his will through his mind. That is, he had the power and the discretion to say, "No, I don't want to climb this tree!" He had the power to decide to climb or not to climb. He was a free moral agent. Remember, there are three spirits: God's Spirit, satan's spirit and your own spirit.

Without an attitude of repentance and faith, God's power cannot work in a man's heart. What does this mean? This means that man's will must be obedient to God's will before he can receive anything from Him.

Zacchaeus' will was obedient to Jesus' will before he received his redemption. He showed an attitude of repentance and faith in Jesus. That was why Jesus' power worked in his heart and he received redemption. That was why he was able to make up his mind. He did not say, "I'm too short to see Jesus", nor did he consider himself a man too rich to climb a tree. He did not bother himself with any of these considerations.

Zacchaeus yielded to God by climbing the tree in order to gain Jesus' attention. That was his vision at that moment. His vision was, "If I can raise myself above everyone, I will gain the attention of Jesus." That was his desire as he saw Jesus coming. "I want to see this man", he must have said in his heart. "...but being a short man he could not..." LUKE 19:3 As a man of vision, being a short man could not stop him from reaching his goal.

Today, there are many factors that influence your will. The factor that could have influenced Zacchaeus' will was his natural circumstance of birth - he was short from birth. For an example, you want to be a soldier but when you go for a medical test, you fail to measure up because you are not physically fit. You want to be a pilot but you cannot see far. In your own life, it could be a natural circumstance of birth such as sickness, disease, poverty, fear or doubt. Zacchaeus was born a short man but that could not change his destiny.

There is nothing to discourage you from reaching God. If Zacchaeus could not be discouraged, there is no reason why you should be discouraged. So, move on. Why should anyone be accused of murder and yet move on? Moses was a murderer but that could not stop his vision. Remember King David. When the prophet came and said to him, "You are not only a murderer but a fornicator," David said, "Oh Lord, what shall I do?" (see **2 SAMUEL 12:7-13**) The Bible says he removed his coat of kingship and begged for forgiveness (see **PSALM 51**). His difficulty improved him. Our difficulties are to improve us. David came out stronger.

Everyone is born with various stigmas. You have your own stigma but that should not stop you from moving on.

Today, many people blame their situation on their family backgrounds. Some will say, "I am poor because everyone in my family is poor."

If you make an excuse for being poor, your poverty cannot be excused.

You are responsible for what you give your attention to. So, it is unnecessary to blame your situation on anyone. In the same way, you are responsible for your own actions. Today it is common for people to blame their failure on their family backgrounds but to attribute their success to their personal effort. If you attribute your success to your personal effort, you should also accept the blame for your failure.

When we make excuses for our wrongdoing, our wrongdoing will not be excused. For an example, I found myself in a family background that irritated me in those early years of my life. I knew I would be blamed for what I gave my attention to. So, I took a different direction in order to achieve a different solution by recognising that victory obtained through Christ Jesus is a time past victory. I mean, it is victory assured. Rather than despair and blame my situation on my family background, I began to be proud of my situation in order to feel Christ's victory over me.

I became content with my situation, knowing that it was redeemable through Christ Jesus and that redemption is a time past redemption - I mean a redemption assured.

I began to take God at His Word in order to have His way. Remember, no one is too good or too bad to qualify for His grace. It was possible for me to sit somewhere and begin to make excuses for my situation, as a free moral agent.

Zacchaeus had the power to choose whom he would serve: to serve satan and remain in that deplorable state or to serve God and receive redemption. In other words, man can decide to yield himself to either God or the devil. Whoever you yield yourself to obey, that is whose servant you are (see ROMANS 6:16).

Whatever I am today is a product of the conviction that victory through Christ is victory indeed. The rest is history.

PRAYER POINTS

O Holy Spirit who reconciles all things in Christ, reconcile me now!

Ask Jesus to take you from where you are now to where HE wants you to be.

STUDY QUESTIONS

ONE// Zacchaeus was a wealthy man – he had position and status. What made him forget all that and climb a tree in the midst of a crowd?

TWO// What makes God's power work in a man's heart?

THREE// What is your natural circumstance of birth? Are you allowing it to hinder you from reaching your goal?

FOR FURTHER READING

ROMANS 5:1

DEUTERONOMY 4:29

AMOS 5:4

EPHESIANS 2:8

REVELATIONS 3:20

ACTS 17:27-28

talk

talk what you believe //WHAT YOU BELIEVE

WORDS TO MEDITATE ON DAY AND NIGHT//PROPHET
MEDITATION BRINGS REVELATION//T.B. JOSHUA

"By an attitude of repentance and faith, man can receive God's blessings, grace, and forgiveness." // LUKE 18:13-14

"If you are in faith, you are not satisfied by the world but look beyond it. This is what the Bible means by, 'You are in the world but not part of it'." // JOHN 17:16

"It is not too late to start believing and obeying the Words of God." // LUKE 19:1-9

"The Bible says that // JOHN 3:2-3
you must be reborn by // 2 CORINTHIANS 6:16
a spiritual miracle to
become a member of the
true Church of
Jesus Christ."

"When you are face to // LUKE 19:1-10
face with Jesus, HE is
not interested in your
attire, position or your
background, but in
your faith because this
is what makes you one
with Him."

The Man At The Beautiful Gate
ACTS 3:1-8

the man at the beautiful gate
ACTS 3:1-8

A look of faith is not just a look, but a look born of God.

"One day Peter and John were going up to the temple at the time of prayer – at three in the afternoon. Now a man crippled from birth was being carried to the temple gate called Beautiful, where he was put every day to beg from those going into the temple courts. When he saw Peter and John about to enter, he asked them for money. Peter looked straight at him, as did John. Then Peter said, 'Look at us!' So the man gave them

his attention, expecting to get something from them."
ACTS 3:1-5

He saw Peter and John about to enter and asked them for money. Peter looked straight at him and said, "Look at us", and the man gave Peter his attention, expecting to get something from them. Peter, as a man of faith, said to the crippled man, "Look at us!" This was not just a look which anybody could look. The look Peter was referring to was not just a look but a look born of faith. A look born of faith is a look born of God.

The need of the crippled man on the outside was silver and gold. Assuming the crippled man had looked on the outside of Peter he would have just seen a fisherman, and what could a fisherman offer? A fisherman has nothing to offer. Assuming he was not looking at Peter on the inside, this kind of look would not have been a look born of faith. Remember, anyone can pray, but only prayers of faith attract Jesus' attention. Many people cry, "Man of God, help me!" Anyone can cry, but only a cry born of faith can attract the man of God.

PRAYER POINTS

The man at the Beautiful Gate was crippled when Peter and John met him.

"Then Peter said, 'Silver or gold I do not have, but what I have I give you. In the name of Jesus Christ of Nazareth, walk!' " ACTS 3:6

After his miracle, he began to walk.

Say, "Every department of my life that is crippled every department of my life that has stopped – walk!' There are many things in your life that are crippled Be it in your business - walk! Be it in your finances, marriage, family, health – walk!

Everything about the man at the Beautiful Gate had stopped before Peter met him. Anything in every department of your life that has stopped – move in Jesus' name! Walk in Jesus' name!

STUDY QUESTIONS

ONE// Had anyone ever prayed for the crippled man's

healing before his encounter with Peter and John?

TWO// Why did Peter ask the crippled man to look at them?

THREE// Peter's name was constantly mentioned. What role did John play then?

FOR FURTHER READING
ISAIAH 35:6
MATTHEW 15:30
ACTS 8:7
ACTS 4:10

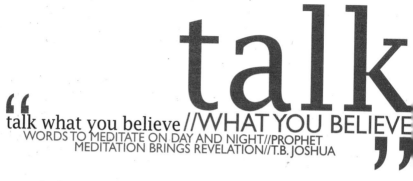

"talk what you believe //WHAT YOU BELIEVE
WORDS TO MEDITATE ON DAY AND NIGHT//PROPHET
MEDITATION BRINGS REVELATION//T.B. JOSHUA"

"A look of faith is to // ACTS 14:8-10
know what God says
about the situation."

"When you express the // LUKE 5:17-20
necessary faith, you
are transformed from
sickness to health."

"What a means of // MATTHEW 9:27-30
blessing is the look of
faith to Christ Jesus.
There is healing, light,
life, in fact everything."

stephen

Stephen was conscious of his faith even in the face of threats to life. ACTS 7:54-60

"When they heard this, they were furious and gnashed their teeth at him. But Stephen, full of the Holy Spirit, looked up to heaven and saw the glory of God, and Jesus standing at the right hand of God. 'Look,' he said, 'I see heaven open and the Son of Man standing at the right hand of God.' At this they covered their ears and, yelling at the top of their voices, they all rushed at him, dragged him out of the city and began to stone him. Meanwhile, the witnesses laid their clothes at the feet of a young man named Saul. While they were stoning him, Stephen prayed, 'Lord Jesus, receive my spirit.' Then he fell on his knees and cried out, 'Lord, do not hold this sin against them.' When he had said this, he fell asleep." ACTS 7:54-60

The Bible says the fear of being stoned did not scare Stephen to abandon his faith and his cause. He was conscious of his faith even in death. The more he was stoned, the stronger he became in his belief, faith and conviction and the more he confessed, "Jesus is the Lord. Jesus is the Redeemer. Jesus is the Saviour". He saw his pain as a reason for believing God, just as he would his good times. What he needed to go free was to recant his belief. Yet at each stone cast on Stephen, the Bible says he confessed, "Jesus is Lord!"

However in your case today, when your trouble is so much, instead of praying the more, you get discouraged and bow to the pressure of the problem. The more your problems: the more you are discouraged, the more you blaspheme, the more you condemn, the more you say, "Jesus be cursed". The more your trials, persecution, isolation and loneliness: the more your grumbling, the more your self-pity, the more your complaint, the more you begin to see Jesus in a bad light.

You are never conscious of your faith when there is pressure, tension or sickness. Remember, as a Christian, problems are meant for your belief. Yet instead of praying the more and having faith the more, you get discouraged.

You allow yourself to be defeated under the weight of the problem. Stephen was able to withstand the stoning because his focus was on his dream of salvation, not on the happenings on the outside. When your focus is on your dream, whatever happens around you will not matter to you (see ACTS 7:55-58).

"His speech persuaded them. They called the apostles in and had them flogged. Then they ordered them not to speak in the name of Jesus, and let them go. The apostles left the Sanhedrin, rejoicing because they had been counted worthy of suffering disgrace for the Name. Day after day, in the temple courts and from house to house, they never stopped teaching and proclaiming the good news that Jesus is the Christ." ACTS 5:40-42

In the face of threats to life, one could continue doing one's assignment for God's sake if one is led by the Holy Spirit. When the Holy Spirit is involved, you will suffer in His way and time. When the apostles were beaten, instead of them to despair, they were happy. They were encouraged because they saw it as a rare privilege to suffer for Christ. They did not preach themselves but Christ; what they heard, they preached. This was the preaching that offended the priests, Pharisees and Saducees.

PRAYER POINTS

Ask God to give you the grace to be conscious of your faith even in the face of threats to life, in Jesus' name.

Say, "Lord Jesus, give me a vision that will impart into me the strength to endure my present situation, in Your holy name."

STUDY QUESTIONS

ONE// Stephen was able to withstand the stoning because his focus was on his dream of salvation. What is your dream?

TWO// While being stoned Stephen saw Jesus standing at the right hand of God. How can we, as Christians, focus our eyes on God who is unseen?

FOR FURTHER READING
I PETER 1:6-7
I TIMOTHY 6:12-16
MARK 13:11
2 CORINTHIANS 4:16-18
MATTHEW 10:39
I PETER 4:16

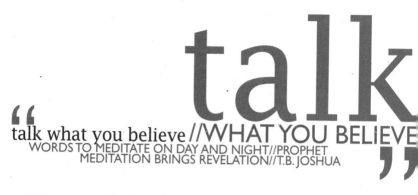

talk

talk what you believe //WHAT YOU BELIEVE
WORDS TO MEDITATE ON DAY AND NIGHT//PROPHET
MEDITATION BRINGS REVELATION//T.B. JOSHUA

"Every true believer in   // JOHN 14:1-3
Christ Jesus can look
forward to a happy life
up in Heaven above."

"If you love God above   // PHILIPPIANS 3:3-11
all, your belief in Him
will see beyond every
other thing."

"The moment you stay   // HEBREWS 12:1-2
in faith, you can hear
from Jesus and know
that all of Heaven is
backing you up."

"By faith, hear Jesus praying for you. By faith, see Jesus looking at you." // HEBREWS 7:25
// PSALM 121:5

"When you are staying in faith in Christ Jesus, you are sitting next to Him on a seat of power with power." // EPHESIANS 2:4-6

"When you speak the name, Jesus Christ, in faith you find yourself in the world of truth." // JOHN 17:15-17

"When we look on the outside of our situation, it always brings fear, worry, and anxiety but a look of faith brings improvement." // ACTS 7:54-60

The Ethiopian Eunuch
ACTS 8:26-39

the ethio- pian

Even though the Ethiopian Eunuch knew that what he wanted to know was not possible without a guide, he was not discouraged.

eunuch
ACTS 8:26-39

"Then the Spirit said to Philip, 'Go near and overtake this chariot.' So Philip ran to him, and heard him reading the prophet Isaiah, and said, 'Do you understand what you are reading?' And he said, 'How can I, unless someone guides me?' And he asked Philip to come up and sit with him."
ACTS 8:29-31 NKJV

While the Ethiopian

Eunuch was busy thinking of his inability to understand the book of Isaiah, little did he know that Somebody was busy planning his enlightenment. That person is the Holy Spirit (see ACTS 8:26).

One thing is clear: man must first show a genuine desire. The Ethiopian Eunuch showed a genuine willingness. The Lord knew his weakness and also his genuine desire: he was desirous to know God better through the written Word of God. He knew that what he wanted to know was difficult to achieve without a guide and that it could only be received by faith.

This situation had to do with his willingness and God's ability. The Ethiopian Eunuch was willing to know more about God. He had a genuine desire. "How can I understand unless someone guides me?" he asked. Even though he knew that what he wanted to know was not possible without a guide, he was not discouraged. He continued reading until the guide came. He had a genuine desire to know more about God, to know what many did not know. Many in his position, without a vision, would have just given up. The Bible says many are called, few are chosen (see

MATTHEW 22:14). People without a vision would give up, but the Ethiopian Eunuch continued to strive after the truth. "To strive" means to struggle. Even though he knew that what he wanted to know was difficult to come by without a guide, he continued to strive. He continued reading until Philip came to help. This is a good example of a genuine desire. Assuming the Ethiopian Eunuch had given up on the situation, what would have happened?

God would have seen him as an unserious mind. The whole world, including Philip, would have seen him the same way. You have to play your own role and God will send someone to help. The Ethiopian Eunuch never gave up to his situation, as many give up to their situations today. Your situation could be trials, temptations or crises.

He kept on reading what he could not read without a guide. He knew he needed a guide who was coming to enlighten him. You can only do what you don't know how to do when you know God will send someone along to guide you.

ONE// If you are looking for counselling,
    follow Jesus; HE is your Counsellor.

TWO// If you are looking for guidance,
    follow Jesus; HE is your Guide.

THREE// If you are looking for healing,
    follow Jesus; HE is your Healer.

FOUR// If you are looking for a teacher,
    follow Jesus; HE is your Teacher.

FIVE// If you are looking for a preacher,
    follow Jesus; HE is your Preacher.

SIX// If you are looking for deliverance,
    follow Jesus; HE is your Deliverer.

SEVEN// If you are looking for redemption,
    follow Jesus; HE is your Redeemer.

EIGHT// If you are looking for friendship,
    follow Jesus; HE is your Friend.

NINE// If you are looking for partnership,
    follow Jesus; HE is your Partner.

TEN// If you are looking for companionship,
    follow Jesus; HE is your Companion.

PRAYER POINTS

Lord Jesus, if their faith is not enough, Father, add to it!

Receive it, in Jesus' name!

Somebody is busy planning your healing. Stop talking about your sickness. Somebody is busy planning your success. Stop talking about your failure. Somebody is busy planning your freedom. Stop talking about your bondage. Somebody is busy planning your deliverance!

The Lord sent Philip to the Ethiopian Eunuch. If the Lord sent me to you, let the Spirit of success continue to locate you! Let the Spirit of victory continue to locate you! And let the Spirit of freedom continue to locate you, in Jesus' name!

STUDY QUESTIONS

ONE// Why did the Ethiopian Eunuch keep reading what he did not understand?

TWO// What was it about Philip that convinced the Ethiopian Eunuch to listen to him? Did he know that Philip was a man of God?

THREE// If you read a Scripture that you struggle to understand, who do you look to for explanation?

FOR FURTHER READING
JOHN 16:13
JOHN 14:26
PSALM 119:34
PSALM 25:5

talk what you believe//WHAT YOU BELIEVE

" WORDS TO MEDITATE ON DAY AND NIGHT//PROPHET
MEDITATION BRINGS REVELATION//T.B. JOSHUA "

"Before your belief can //I CORINTHIANS 12:3
be genuine, your faith
must be born of the
Holy Spirit."

"Believing in Jesus // JOHN 1:12
Christ is the answer to
the human dilemma."

"The best way to get // ROMANS 10:17
faith is to hear the
Words of God. It is
important to hear not
only with our ears but
also with our hearts."

"If you must have   // I THESSALONIANS 2:13
faith, you must learn
to hear God's Word.
Because through
hearing, belief comes.
Through believing,
trust comes. Through
trusting, confidence is
established."

"You are not saved   // EPHESIANS 2:8
because you feel saved;
you are saved because
you have put your faith
in God's Word and acted
on it."

"Our evidence for what   // JOSHUA 6:2-21
we believe is our faith in
God's Word."

bodily pains counted for nothing. Instead of the beating and humiliation they received in the hands of the Roman officials and the mob, making them abandon their cause (I mean their faith), it made them have faith the more, pray the more, believe the more and praise God the more. The more they were beaten, humiliated and embarrassed, the more their faith, belief and conviction about Jesus Christ.

When Paul and Silas were chained to the ground, they began to sing praises to the Lord. They saw their suffering as a reason for their belief, just as they saw their freedom.

They were conscious of their faith even under the serious pressure and threat to their lives. They were expected to say, "We are very sorry; we will not mention the name, Jesus, again".

Ordinarily, their situation did not call for thanksgiving
r praise. They were praising God while being chained
nds and feet. When you are face to face with Jesus,
is not interested in your appearance, position,
'her you are a king, queen, president or secretary

paul & silas

ACTS 16:20-25

Paul and Silas chose the bright colour of praise instead of the dark colours of depression, bitterness, despair, self-pity and rejection.

"Upon receiving such orders, he put them in the inner cell and fastened their feet in the stocks. About midnight Paul and Silas were praying and singing hymns to God, and the other prisoners were listening to them. Suddenly there was such a violent earthquake that the foundations of the prison were shaken. At once all the prison doors flew open, and everybody's chains came loose." ACTS 16:24-26

In the case of Paul and Silas,

general. HE is only interested in your faith because that is what makes you one with Him.

When Paul and Silas were imprisoned at Philippi and their backs were raw from beatings, they sang hymns (see ACTS 16:23-25). They chose the bright colour of praise instead of the dark colours of depression, bitterness, despair, self-pity and rejection. No matter what affliction or crisis we may face, we too can decide how we respond.

Apostle Paul was conscious of his faith even under pressure and tension. Daniel was conscious of his faith even under pressure and tension. Shadrach, Meshach and Abednego were conscious of their faith even under pressure and tension. What they needed to go free was to say, "I am sorry, Oh King. We will worship your god and your god will be our god". On the contrary, they were conscious of their faith so they stayed true to their God, even under serious pressure and the threat to their lives.

PRAYER POINTS

Ask God to give you the grace to be conscious of your faith even under pressure and tension, in Jesus' name.

When Paul and Silas were in prison, the angel of God visited them and the foundations of the prison were shaken. The angel of God wants to visit you right now. He is on his way.

The foundation and pillar of your problem, crumble, in Jesus' name!

Right now, it is time to take all the breakthrough keys. The book of MATTHEW 16:19 says, "I will give you the keys of the kingdom of heaven; whatever you bind on earth will be bound in heaven, and whatever you loose on earth will be loosed in heaven." The Lord promised to give you keys to loose whatever has been bound in your life - breakthrough keys to your finances and your marital bliss.

Continue to take all the breakthrough keys - keys to loose and keys to bind. Whatever might have been bound, be loosed in Jesus' name; whatever might have been loosed, be bound in Jesus' name!

STUDY QUESTIONS

ONE// Paul and Silas were the innocent victims in the prison. Yet, when they were praising their God, why were all the prisoners set free?

TWO// Paul and Silas were in the dark in the inner cell. How did Paul know that the jailer who was far from them wanted to kill himself (see ACTS 16:27-29)?

THREE// Put yourself in Paul and Silas' position. When the situation seems unfavourable to you, does your desire to praise God become stronger?

FOUR// Paul and Silas did not murmur or rebel but praised God the more and an entire household was saved. Do people accept Jesus Christ upon seeing the way you handle your tests and trials?

FOR FURTHER READING
I PETER 4:12-16; PSALM 34:1-3
HEBREWS 13:15; PSALM 51:15; ACTS 12:5-10

talk what you believe // WHAT YOU BELIEVE

WORDS TO MEDITATE ON DAY AND NIGHT//PROPHET
MEDITATION BRINGS REVELATION//T.B. JOSHUA

"Everyone can clap after // JOHN 11:40-44
a miracle, but it takes
faith to clap before
the miracle."

"When we worship God // JOHN 4:23-24
in faith and in truth,
we put ourselves in a
position that attracts
His attention and
commitment. When we
attract His attention and
commitment, we begin
to enjoy His promises."

"**If you handle your hard** // PSALM 30:5
times with care, they
will soon become
good times."

"When something is out // ACTS 16:24-25
of order, begin to lift up
your hands and sing to
the Holy Spirit. I mean
begin to sing louder and
become aggressive in
your worship."

"**In the process of** // JAMES 1:12
practising your faith,
there may be some
unpleasant situations
- endure them."

CONGRATULATIONS!

You have finished your reading of this book, **The Mirror**. Kindly accept my congratulations. Remember, however, that as Christians, our road map is the Bible. The more we read it with devotion, the more effective we will be for God. We must approach God's Word as if our lives depended on it. The Word of God will build your faith. Faith will grow as you continually hear God's Word.

The Bible says whoever desires can be saved (see REVELATION 22:17). Obviously, any person who hears God's Word and acts on it can exercise faith. People who neither hear God's Word nor obey it do not have God's kind of faith. Faith requires hearing and obeying so that we may be delivered from unreasonable and wicked men, for not all have faith (see 2 THESSALONIANS 3:2). You therefore have to do the following:

ONE// read your Bible daily,
TWO// read it because it is food for your soul,
THREE// read it because it is a guide for your feet,
FOUR// read it because it is very profitable,

FIVE// read it to keep you from error and sin,
SIX// read it because it has healing
power and,
SEVEN// read it because it has a purifying power.

WHAT YOU NEED TO DO

Pray for your church that your pastors, deacons, evangelists and all the members may be filled with the Holy Spirit and be used by Him.

Discuss with your pastor, teacher or friend about what you have gained from **The Mirror**.

THE POWER OF FAITH

What is the power of faith? Read the following for an answer:

ONE// MARK 9:23

TWO// HEBREWS 11:6

THREE// GALATIANS 3:14

FOUR// JAMES 5:15

FIVE// EPHESIANS 2:8

One of the best chapters in the entire Bible on the subject of faith is the 11th chapter of Hebrews. I suggest the chapter to be read as you read the words in this book on the subject of faith.

Finally, I would like to congratulate you again on the success you have achieved so far in completing your reading of this book, **The Mirror**. God bless you. Amen.

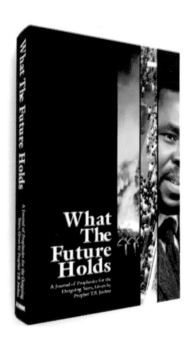

WHAT THE FUTURE HOLDS

A journal of prophecies for the outgoing years, given by Prophet T.B. Joshua regarding the events which were to come concerning indviduals, nations and the world at large - revealing to all that Jesus Christ holds our future.

Men spoke the message of God as they were carried along by the Holy Spirit. As it was, so it is.

We must be under the check and conduct of the Holy Spirit. God's Word must be our rule and His grace must be our principle to know what the future holds.

www.scoan.com/store

DAILY TIME WITH GOD

Are you spending your time with the right source? Are you spending your DAILY TIME WITH GOD? This devotional handbook by Prophet T.B. Joshua will show you that if you spend your time with Jesus Christ, it will be well spent. As you read this pocket-sized devotional book, let God talk to you daily, through His Word, by His Spirit. Each full-colour, illustrated page is filled with words of wisdom and Scripture that will shift your relationship with God to another level. Remember, when God talks, the wise listen. When you open the Bible and read with devotion you are hearing God talk.

www.scoan.com/store

Emmanuel TV is a new satellite television station dedicated to changing lives, changing nations and changing the world.

Emmanuel TV is broadcast on:
- PanAmSat PAS10, which covers the whole of sub-Saharan Africa as well as Europe, and,
- Intelsat Americas 5, which covers all of the United States, Canada, Mexico and the Caribbean.

If millions of this generation are to believe in Jesus, they must see proof that Jesus Christ is the same yesterday, today and forever (see Hebrews 13:8).

The Emmanuel TV team is using this opportunity to congratulate TBN, The GOD Channel, The Hope Channel, Daystar and other channels we are not able to mention, on their contribution towards saving souls and bringing many sons unto the glory of Jesus Christ.

Emmanuel TV – what a rare privilege to preach the Gospel of our Lord Jesus Christ across the world!

The Synagogue, Church Of All Nations, Lagos, Nigeria, is the headquarters of the international ministry of Prophet T.B. Joshua.

We welcome visitors from across the globe to stay with us and witness first-hand proof that the age of miracles has not past; the Miracle Worker is still alive; His name is Jesus Christ!

For further details about visiting us, church accommodation, meals and transportation, please view our website: www.scoan.com or contact: info@scoan.com; synagogue@themaninthesynagogue.org

Nigeria: +234 (0) 706 486 5517
          +234 (0) 705 807 9083
UK: +44 (0) 2070603939